FATHERS, FAMILIES,
AND THE OUTSIDE WORLD

Winnicott Studies Monograph Series

Edited by Val Richards

The Person Who Is Me:
Contemporary Perspectives on the True and False Self

The Squiggle Foundation is a registered charity
set up in 1981 to study and cultivate the tradition
of D. W. Winnicott. For further information, contact
The Administrator, 33 Amberley Road, London N13 4BH.
Tel: 0181 882 9744; Fax: 0181 886 2418

Winnicott Studies Monograph Series

FATHERS, FAMILIES, AND THE OUTSIDE WORLD

edited by
Val Richards

with
Gillian Wilce

London
KARNAC BOOKS
for
The Squiggle Foundation

First published in 1997 by
H. Karnac (Books) Ltd.
58 Gloucester Road
London SW7 4QY

British Library Cataloguing in Publication Data

A C.I.P. for this book is available from the British Library

ISBN 1 85575 170 4

Edited, designed, and produced by Communication Crafts

Printed in Great Britain by BPC Wheatons Ltd, Exeter

10 9 8 7 6 5 4 3 2 1

CONTENTS

ACKNOWLEDGEMENTS

The Editors wish to thank the following people for their valuable support and advice:

Editorial Committee: Jan Abram, Sheila Ernst, Nina Farhi, Wille Henriques, Amelie Noack, Rosie Parker, Margaret Walters, Lindsay Wells

The Trustees of The Squiggle Foundation

Karnac Books: Cesare Sacerdoti, Graham Sleight

CONTRIBUTORS

JOHN FIELDING is Head of English at the Lycée Français, with a particular interest in teaching and directing the plays of Shakespeare and in the overlap between literature and psychoanalysis. He has been associated with the Squiggle Foundation from its beginning and is a regular presenter at its seminars and public events.

JOHN FORRESTER is Reader in History and Philosophy of the Sciences at the University of Cambridge. He has written extensively on psychoanalysis, including *Language and the Origins of Psychoanalysis* (1980), *The Seductions of Psychoanalysis: Freud, Lacan and Derrida* (with Lisa Appignanesi, 1990), *Freud's Women* (1992), and *Dispatches from the Freud Wars—Psychoanalysis and Its Passions* (1997). The author also co-translated and edited Lacan's *Seminars I and II*. His latest book, *Truth Game: Lies, Money and Psychoanalysis*, will be published in late 1997.

GRAHAM LEE is a psychoanalytic psychotherapist and an Associate Member of the Association for Group and Individual Psychotherapy. As a complement to his private practice, he acts as a consultant to organizations, drawing on psychodynamic ideas within his approach to business psychology and management development.

VAL RICHARDS is a psychoanalytic psychotherapist, the editor of Winnicott Studies, and an Assistant Director of the Squiggle Foundation. She is a Member of the Institute of Psychotherapy and Social Studies and the Guild of Psychotherapists and teaches on various trainings. Her publications include "The Lac-king" (in Shakespeare and the Changing Curriculum, 1990), book reviews in the British Journal of Psychotherapy, and papers in previous Winnicott Studies.

FATHERS, FAMILIES,
AND THE OUTSIDE WORLD

Introduction:
Papa versus Pooh

> [The child] is also looking for his father, one might say, who will protect mother when she is found. The strict father that the child evokes may also be loving, but he must first be strict and strong. Only when the strict and strong father figure is in evidence can the child regain his primitive love impulses, his sense of guilt, and his wish to mend. [Winnicott, 1946, p. 116]

Here, at first sight, is Winnicott's portrayal of the father as strong and masterful, with the primary task of protecting the mother by coming between her and her tempestuous child. In providing a strong framework for the child's containment, this father continues and extends the primary maternal holding by restoring the "bad-enough child" to itself. But alongside this strong, stern evocation, there seems to lurk a more passive and backward-looking paternal figure, who shirks the task of propelling his offspring into the domain of difference and of language. For, as is brought out in both Fielding's and Forrester's chapters in this monograph, it is as if all the dynamism

1

and initiative of the father is seized by Winnicott himself, in his Prosper(o)ing practice. This leaves the theoretical father somewhat shorn of his phallic, oedipal role.

If, with Winnicott's post-oedipal child, the father's main job is to take over from the mother the key job of holding and containment, such a containing, protective function begins to look almost recursive, pointing backwards to the child's rediscovery of mother: "[The child] is also looking for his father, one might say, who will protect mother when she is found." It is perhaps Winnicott's preoccupation with this rearguard action of the father that leads him to pay scant attention to the latter's role as initiator of the child into the symbolic order. It reflects Winnicott's attachment to the "realness", the special authenticity, of the early pre-verbal stages, the spontaneity and "directness" of the infant's communication with m/other, which almost suggest that the father–language, when it comes, is a bit of an interloper. As expressed in "Communicating and Not Communicating Leading to a Study of Certain Opposites" (1963a), language is secondary, an accretion, and other, earlier ways of communicating are implicitly better, because more direct:

> By the time mothers have become objectively perceived their infants have become masters of various techniques for indirect communication, the most obvious of which is the use of language. [p. 188]

Although the centrality of symbol formation is conceptualized in Winnicott's theory of transitional phenomena, in its most developed form of language (linked theoretically to sexual difference), he does not stress that language is as crucial for the *continuing* formation of identity as is the primal mirror/milk experience.

According to Winnicott, the primary achievement of symbol formation is the internalization of the mother and the management of emotions around her absence—the lack of the object and the *need* for relationship. Indeed, has not the Winnicottian infant already, before the descent of the father, virtually negotiated the advent of the symbolic, of difference and loss, by means of the transitional object? Is there not a sense in which this crucial distance from the world of oneness and sameness to a world of plurality and difference has already been travelled, enacted between mother, child, and, say, Pooh, rather than between mother, child, and Papa? It sometimes seems that when Winnicott's theoretical father arrives in the nursery, his task has already been accomplished—by a toy—and everything that could ever matter has already happened. As expressed by Adam Phillips (1988, p. 28) and quoted by John Fielding in chapter three, "It is not the father that interests Winnicott as coming between the mother and child to separate them, but a transitional space from which the father is virtually absent".

A comparison of Winnicott's conceptualization of the father as a disturber of nursery idyll—the father who "must first be strict and strong"—with that of the law-bringing father of Lacan sheds light on this gap in Winnicott's thought, for the Lacanian law-giving father comes also as a bearer of gifts: specifically the gift of language, which will contribute vitally to the continued shaping of identity. In the work of Lacan, we see theorized the tie between the advent of the father at the oedipal stage and the subject's insertion into the symbolic order of language, as Eagleton (1985) indicated:

> For the drama of the Oedipus complex to come about at all, the child must . . . have become dimly aware of sexual difference. It is the entry of the father which signifies this sexual difference. . . . It is only by accepting the necessity of sexual difference, of distinct gender roles, that the child, who has previously been unaware of such problems, can become properly "socialised". Lacan's originality is to rewrite this process, which we have already seen in Freud's account of the Oedipus complex, in terms of language. . . . With the entry of the father, the child . . . now has to grasp Saussure's point that identities come about only as a result of difference—that one term or subject is only what it is by excluding another. Significantly, the child's first discovery of sexual difference occurs at about the same time that it is discovering language itself. [pp. 165–166]

The difference in emphasis is clarified by the example of Freud's "Fort Da" game (1920). From the elevation of the perambulator, Freud's grandson repeatedly hurled to the ground a cotton-reel on a string, crying "Gone!", and then hauled it back, triumphantly shouting "Here!" For Winnicott (and other object relations theorists), this is seen primarily as demonstrating the child's capacity to symbolize by forming an internal image of the vanished mother, which enables him to express confidence in her expected return.

But the scene can also be re-interpreted less in terms of object relating and more in terms of the symbolic as *language*, of the magical grasp and conversion of absence into presence by the utterance of a verbal sound. Then comfort and satisfaction come less from the *image* of the missing other than from possession of the whole new dimension of language:

> [In Freud's Fort Da game], the real mother disappeared and the child put to the test the magic power of the word (the mother disappeared but the word remained). . . .
>
> The child . . . punctuated with a word what could be interpreted as the rejection and return of the mother. The words "gone" and "here" introduced a third dimension—beyond the absence of the real mother, the child found the Symbolic mother by means of a word. [Mannoni, 1967, pp. 17, 19]

This realization that language plays a liberating and empowering role in the ongoing formation of identity contributes to the allied recognition that, far from being "settled" in early infancy, the self is never immune from later damage and insult. Yet, as part of Winnicott's vision of the self, set up for better or worse with its primal mother's milk and mirroring, it is as if only this original primal self is really true and enduring. The major implication of this is that little room is allowed either for further psychic development or for those traumas to the self and inevitable reactions to impingements that can occur at any stage in life, on the heels of the oedipal stage and the recognition of difference.

It is not that Winnicott disputes or denies the possibility, despite good-enough mothering, of later trauma to the self. Indeed, the almost mystical vision of the core self evoked in "Communicating and Not Communicating" (1963a) seems to require a designated *False* self to shield, in effect, virtually all post-"infans" (infans = "non-speaking") states of being. Thus the core self is sealed off to protect it from penetration by language:

> I suggest that in health there is a core to the personality that corresponds to the true self of the split personality; I suggest that this core never communicates with the world of per-

ceived objects, and that the individual person knows that it must never be communicated with or be influenced by external reality. . . . Each individual is an isolate, permanently non-communicating, permanently unknown, in fact, unfound. . . . Rape, and being eaten by cannibals, these are mere bagatelles as compared with the violation of the self's core, the alteration of the self's central elements by communication seeping through the defences. [p. 187]

It is as if Winnicott's gaze, so irresistibly drawn in the direction of infancy, is (unlike that of Kohut who theorizes the continuing development and vulnerability of the self) too full of the nursery scenario to theorize the advent of the father–language in other than practical terms, as buffer and defender.

To suggest briefly, therefore, how this later factor of language, the Lacanian Law of the Father, is seen as absolutely crucial for the continuing formation of identity and psychological health, the following example quoted by Maude Mannoni (from a study by R. D. Laing) analyses trauma to the self *not* so much in terms of failed maternal mirroring and faded internal objects, but more in terms of the self's abject dependence on being held together by the *linguistic structures* that it has absorbed from its first parents. This material illustrates the important point that the self may never be immune from violation, for notice that the child involved is not an infant but is 4 years old.

> The case was that of a four-year-old boy called Brian who was taken by his mother to meet a couple who were to adopt him. The mother kissed her child, burst into tears, and ran out without a word. Brian never saw her again. . . . [The couple] tried to establish themselves for him by saying, "You are our son." But the child would not accept it. He became difficult and, gradually, completely maladjusted.
>
> Brian no longer knew *who he was*. . . . His first identity was that of being the son of his mother. . . . [H]e awaited her return to be sure again who he was. . . . But . . . he did know *what he was*: he was wicked because his mother had got rid of him. . . .
>
> In the past which linked Brian to his mother, he had her words that defined him as her son. . . . He then had to build his life on the basis of words that had been foreclosed. "You are our son," said his adopted parents, but the mother rendered the transition impossible by never having indicated to

him in words that he was no longer her child. . . . [T]he adults forgot the words of the past which remained inscribed in the child's unconscious and continued to produce effects at the level of the symptom. The traumatic situation can be understood only by reference to the mother's doubletalk. [Mannoni, 1967, pp. 12–13]

The claim here is that the self's formation and survival are inextricably bound up with the verbal meanings initially conveyed to the young child by the original parents, and the original mother's mystifying silence, her absence of explanation, and her disappearance rendered the information from the new parents—"You are *our* son"—completely double-binding. It is such insults to identity, once the child is established in verbal understanding, that can cause a later fracturing of the so far intact, untorn self. While this case can be seen in terms solely of object loss and separation trauma, it appears that the agony is in no small measure inextricably tied up with the formation of the child's identity by the word of the adult, established by the intervention of the theoretical third/father.

Turning now to the father featured in the Winnicott paper on delayed reaction to loss, reprinted here in chapter one: the hero of the story is a dead, drowned father, who apparently gave his life for his son Patrick. As brought out in John Forrester's commentary in chapter two, "On Holding as a Metaphor", when the boy is brought to him for treatment Winnicott seizes the paternal lawgiving role for himself, imposing *"absolute prohibitions"* on both the surviving son and the bereaved widow. Wearing both his medical and his psychoanalytic hats, he precipitates the boy's necessary illness and orders the mother to postpone mourning for her lost spouse. He expresses no interest in the extraordinary mystery of what actually took place between father and son when they plunged overboard. The vital issue of the father's agency in his son's salvation is subverted by the suggestion that Patrick himself may have played a part in his father's drowning. So the question of who was holding whom remains unexplored, and the only quoted fact about the father is the son's reporting that his father "may have committed suicide". Here Winnicott's holding of the bereaved family takes the form of a tight but remote control, which reflects the stance of Prospero as depicted in John Fielding's study (chapter three).

It seems as though Winnicott—except when assuming the role for himself, as above—is obscurely uncomfortable with the idea of the dynamic, proactive, forward-looking father, preferring perhaps the long-suffering, devoted father, the willing buffer, ready to be buffeted. This is further exemplified in chapter five, "If Father Could Be Home . . .", in the passage quoted from *The Piggle* describing a father who in fact is not so very different from mother.

In this emerging portrait of a strong but passive and backward-looking father, there is surely a link with what I have seen to be Winnicott's theoretical ambivalence towards language and difference. This is echoed in John Fielding's reading of *The Tempest*, and of the function of Prospero, "So Rare a Wonder'd Father" (chapter three), which demonstrates how the master magician subsumes in himself both mother and father roles, while also splitting off into the rejected Caliban the vital formative and creative properties of language, inseparable from progress to three-person relating (Caliban: "You taught me language and my profit on't/I know how to curse"). Psychoanalytically speaking, with no third party to prise a space between child (Miranda) and mother/father (Prospero), there can be no experience of difference—until the apparition of brave-new-world Ferdinand. Only then can Prospero declare of Caliban: "This thing of darkness I acknowledge mine."

But there the resemblance to the Winnicott father, in terms of resistance to difference and the formative role of language, ceases. For, in Fielding's reading, Prospero, as amalgamated mother/father, conforms less to Winnicott's general evocation of paternal *holding* than to that of paternal *control*—"father's almost unfettered power to do and to forbid" Thus, although all the fathers in Prospero's story are saved from drowning by his magic, Patrick's drowned father cannot be reached by Winnicott's magic. Prospero, however, lacking the psychological wizardry of Winnicott himself, proves impotent to *make* his "creatures" feel what he desires them to feel.

The mother/father amalgamation in Prospero, like the implied exclusivity of mother, child, and bear within Winnicott's transitional space, makes way for a fresh perspective in the theoretical contribution of Graham Lee (chapter four). His "Alone Among Three", building on Winnicott's original dyadic transitional space, modulates this into a place where there really is enough room for three. Here, the mother and father are plainly at times enough taken up with one another, and at times enough involved with their child, for the latter to be held in a rhythm of inclusion and exclusion.

Now we are three, the air circulates, the words fly—out of the nursery into the master bedroom. Now there is space for "the bad-enough child" to "challenge the language of the parents" and for the return of the workaday Winnicott father and his clearly appointed role in "the family . . . and the outside world".

Val Richards

CHAPTER ONE

A child psychiatry case illustrating delayed reaction to loss

Written for a collection of essays in memory of Marie Bonaparte, 1965[1]

D. W. Winnicott

On his eleventh birthday Patrick suffered the loss of his father by drowning. The way in which he and his mother needed and used professional help illustrates the function of the psychoanalyst in child psychiatry.

In the course of one year Patrick was given ten interviews and his mother four, and during the four years since the tragedy occurred I have kept in touch, by telephone conversations with the mother, with the boy's clinical state as well as with the mother's management of her son and of herself. The mother started with very little understanding of psychology and with considerable hostility to psychiatrists, and she gradually developed the qualities and insight that were needed. The part she was to play was, in effect, the mental nursing of Patrick during his breakdown. She was very much encouraged by being able to undertake this heavy task and by succeeding in it.

---

[1]*Drives, Affects, Behavior: Essays in Memory of Marie Bonaparte, Vol. 2*, ed. Max Schur (New York: International Universities Press, 1965).

Family

The father had a practice in one of the professions. He had achieved considerable success and had very good prospects. Together they had a large circle of friends.

There were two children of the marriage, a boy at university and Patrick, who was a boarder at a well-known preparatory school. The family had a town house in London and a holiday cottage on an island off the coast. It was in the sea near the holiday cottage that the father was drowned when sailing with Patrick on the day after his eleventh birthday.

The evolution of the psychiatrist's contact with the case

The evolution of the case is given in detail and as accurately as possible because this case illustrates certain features of child psychiatry casework which I consider to be vitally important.

Whenever possible I get at the history of a case by means of psychotherapeutic interviews *with the child*. The history gathered in this way contains the vital elements, and it is of no matter if in certain aspects the history taken in this way proves to be incorrect. The history taken in this way evolves itself, according to the child's capacity to tolerate the facts. There is a minimum of questioning for the sake of tidiness or for the sake of filling in gaps. Incidentally, the diagnosis reveals itself at the same time. By this method one is able to assess the degree of integration of the child's personality, the child's capacity for holding conflicts and strain, the child's defences both in their strength and in their kind, and one can make an assessment of the family and general environmental reliability or unreliability; and, in certain cases, one may discover or pinpoint continuous or continuing environmental insults.

The principles enunciated here are the same as those that characterize a psychoanalytic treatment. The difference between psychoanalysis and child psychiatry is chiefly that in the former one tries to get the chance to do as much as possible (and the psychoanalyst likes to have five or more sessions a week), whereas in the latter one asks: how little need one do? What is lost by doing as little as possible is balanced by an immense gain, since in child psychiatry one has access to a vast number of cases for which (as in the present case) psychoanalysis is not a practical proposition. To my surprise, I find that the child psychiatry case has much to teach the psychoanalyst, though the debt is chiefly in the other direction.

First contact

A woman (who turned out to be Patrick's mother) telephoned out of the blue to say she had reluctantly decided to take the risk of consulting someone about her son, who was at a prep school, and she had been told by a friend that I was probably not as dangerous as most of my kind. I certainly could not have foretold at this initial stage that she would prove capable of seeing her son through a serious illness.

I was told that the father had been drowned in a sailing accident, that Patrick had been to some extent responsible for the tragedy, and that she, the mother, and the older son, were still very disturbed and that the effect on Patrick had been complex. The clinical evidence of disturbance in Patrick had been delayed and it now seemed desirable that someone should investigate. Patrick had always been devoted to his mother, and since the accident had become (what she called) emotional.

In this brief account of a long telephone conversation I have not attempted to reproduce the mother's rush of words or her scepticism in regard to psychiatric services.

First interview with Patrick
(two months after this telephone conversation)

Patrick was brought by his mother. I found him to be of slight build, with a large head. He was obviously intelligent and alert and likeable. I gave him the whole time of the interview (two hours). There was no point in the interview at which the relationship between him and me was difficult. Only during the most tense part of the consultation was it impossible for me to take notes. The following account was written after the interview.

Patrick said he was not doing very well at school, but he "liked intellectual effort". We were seated at a low round table with paper and pencils provided, and we started with the Squiggle Game. (In this I make a squiggle for him to turn into something, and then he makes one for me to do something with.)

1. He made mine into an elephant.
2. He made his own into "a Henry Moore abstract." Here he showed that he was in contact with modern art and later it became clear that this is something which belongs to his relationship to his mother. She takes an active part in keeping him well informed in the art world, which has been important to him since the age of five years. It also shows his sense of humour, which is important prognostically. It shows his toleration of madness and of mutilation and of the macabre. It might be said that it also shows that he has talent as an artist, but this comes out more clearly in a later drawing. His choosing to turn his squiggle into an abstract was related to the danger, very real in his case, that because of his very good intellectual capacity he would escape from emotional tensions into compulsive intellectualization; and because of paranoid fears, which later became

evident, there could be a basis here for an organized system of thought.

3. I turned his squiggle into two figures which he called "mother holding a baby." I did not know at the time that here was already an indication of his main therapeutic need.

4. He turned mine into an artistic production. It was done quickly and he knew exactly what he was doing. He said it was a tree at F. I did not know at that time that F. was the site of the tragedy, but in this drawing there was already incorporated his drive to cope with the problem surrounding his father's death.

5. This is his drawing, done at my request, of the holiday island, with F. shown.

6. He turned his own into "a mother scolding a child," and here

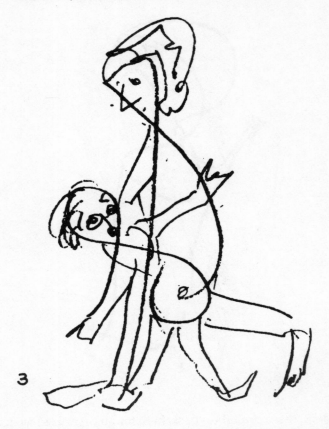

3

one might see something of his wish to be punished by the mother.

7. He turned mine into Droopy.

8. I made his into some kind of a comical girl figure.

9. This was important. He made my squiggle into a sculpture of a rattlesnake. "It might have been by a modern artist", he said. In this case he took hold of a squiggle with all its madness and incontinence and turned it into a work of art, in this way gaining control of impulse that threatens to get out of control.

10. In the next I turned his into some kind of a weird hand, and he said it might be by Picasso. This led to a discussion of Picasso in which he displayed his knowledge of Picasso in a way that sounded a little precocious. We agreed that the recent Picasso

4

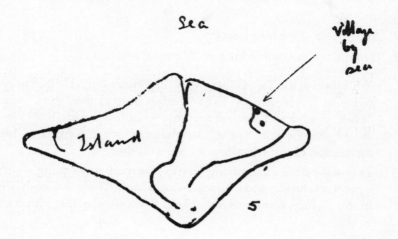

Sea

village
by
sea

Island

5

15

exhibition at the Tate Gallery was very interesting. He had been twice to it. He said he liked Picasso best in the "pink" and "blue" period and seemed to know what this meant, but I was aware that he was talking language which belonged to his discussion of these matters with his mother.

11. This was rather a surprising picture. He made my squiggle into a person who slipped into some dog's food. There is a lot of life in the picture, but I was not able to find out why this idea had

turned up. I would think he was mocking me or perhaps all men.

He then started talking, and drawing became less important. What we talked about included the following:

In the first term at school he had had a dream. He had been ill with some kind of epidemic two nights before half-term, which he said is "an exciting time for a new bug." In the dream the Matron told him to get up and go to the hall where the tramps are fed. The

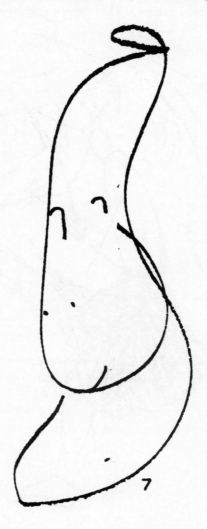

Matron shouted: "Is everyone here?" There were fifteen *but one was missing*; nobody knew that one was missing. It was weird in some way because there was no extra person. And then there was a church with no altar, and a shadow where the altar had been.

The rest had to do with a baby jumping up and down, of which he drew a picture (no. 12). The baby was screaming, going up and down on the mattress. He said that the baby was about 18 months old. I asked him whether he had known babies and he said: "About three." It seemed, however, that he was referring in the dream to his own infancy. This dream remained obscure, but its

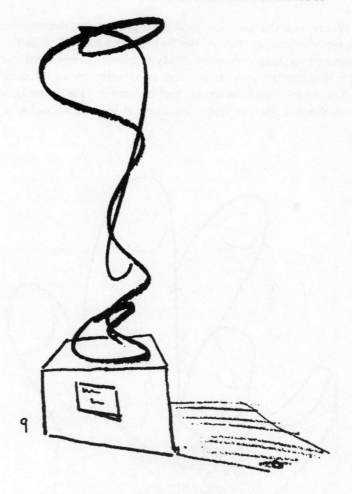

meaning became elucidated in the fourth interview, four weeks later. It was thought that there was a reference to the dead father in the one person missing.

At this stage I did not know that he had not been told at once about his father's death.

13. Here is his drawing of the church with a shadow instead of an altar. I asked: "What would be a nice dream?" He said quickly: "Bliss, being cared for. I know I want this."

When I put the question he said he knew what depression was like, especially since father's death. He had a love of his father, but he did not see him very much. "My father was very kind. But the fact is that mother and father were constantly under tension." He went on to talk about what he had observed: "I was the link that joined them; I tried to help. To father it was outrageous to pre-

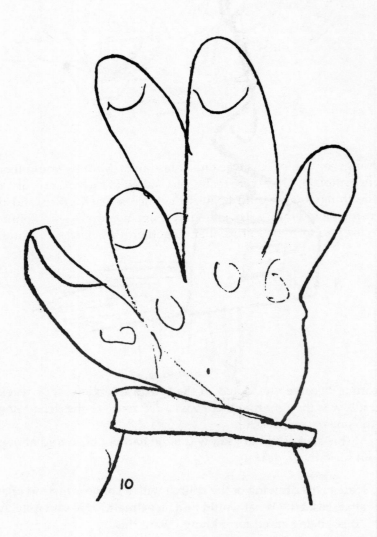

10

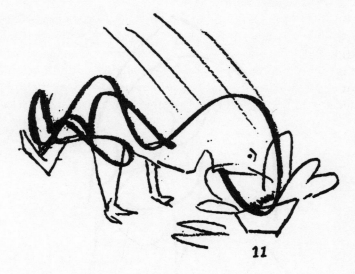

11

arrange anything. This was one of his faults. Mother would therefore complain. They were really very suited to each other, but over
little things they would begin to get across each other, and the
tension would built up over and over again, and the only solution
to this was for me to bring them together. Father was very much

12

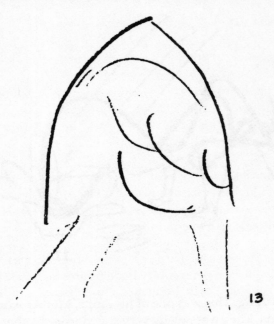

13

overworked. He may not have been very happy. It was a great strain to him to come home tired and then for his wife to fail him." In all this he showed an unusual degree of insight.[2]

The rest of this long and astonishing interview consisted in our going over in great detail the episode in which his father died. He said that his father "may have committed suicide"[3] or perhaps it was his own (Patrick's) fault; it was impossible to know. "After a long time in the water one began to fight for oneself." Patrick had a life belt and the father had none. They were nearly both drowned, but sometime after the father had sunk, just near dark, Patrick was rescued by chance. For some time he did not realize

---

[2]It was this quality in Patrick which made me wish to present this case in Marie Bonaparte's book, because we have clear evidence of the deep insight that was Marie Bonaparte's when she was at the latency stage; see *Five Copy-Books* (London: Imago, 1950).—*D.W.W.*

[3]There is good evidence that neither parent was in fact suicidal.—*D.W.W.*

that his father was dead, and at first he was told that he was in the hospital. Then Patrick said that if his father had lived, he thinks his mother would have committed suicide. "The tension between the two was so great that it was not possible to think of them going on without one of them dying." There was therefore a feeling of relief, and he indicated that he felt very guilty about this. (It will be understood that this is not to be taken as an objective and final picture of the parental relationship. It was true, however, for Patrick.)

At the end he dealt with the very great fears he had had from early childhood. He described his great fear associated with hallucinations both visual and auditory, and *he insisted that his illness, if he was ill, antedated the tragedy.*

14. This is a drawing of Patrick's home with the various places marked in which persecutory male figures appear. The principal danger area was in the lavatory, and there was only one spot for him to use when urinating if he would avoid persecutory hallucinations.

There was a quality about this phobic system that seemed to belong more naturally to an emotional age of 4 rather than to 11 years, with phobias closely linked with hallucinations. The whole matter was discussed in terms of dream life spilling over into the waking life, and along with this the idea of the tragedy as a hallucination and yet real. Patrick described panic as being in a nightmare when awake. The hallucinations he feels are ghosts of a returning vengeful man, but they antedate the tragedy.

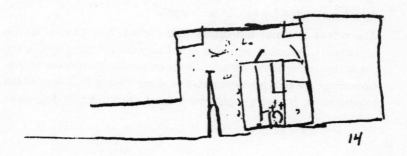

14

It will be noted that a drawing that came with a powerful drive from the unconscious (no. 12) had no meaning for him. I did nothing about it, though it seemed to me to convey a manic defence quality. This proved to be the most significant of the drawings, but I had to wait till the fourth interview (about a month later) to gain a precise understanding of it.

The accent in this interview was on the drowning incident, remembered and described in a rather detached way. After two hours we both had had enough. Probably we both knew there was much more to be done, but we did not say so to each other. The effect on Patrick was that he gained confidence in me, and the effect on myself was that I now knew a good deal about him from inside him.

From this first interview I got a glimpse of the personality and character of the patient. In addition, I learned:

1. Patrick was beginning to feel guilty about the father's death.

2. He did not yet feel sad.

3. He felt threatened by the arrival of feelings that had been so long delayed.

4. He had a fear of illness, and there was a basis for this in the hidden illness dating from early years with a liability to hallucinosis.

5. There was an indication of an important unknown factor represented by the unexplained bouncing baby drawing.

6. At school he had had undefined illnesses for which he had sought the Matron's care. Later I found that he had produced his symptoms deliberately, not knowing how else to get the special and personal care that he needed. This had taken place in the autumn when he was supposedly quite happy and well, and "unaffected by his father's death."

7. There was a strong indication that Patrick had a belief in the existence of reliable persons, and I noted that this faith of his could be used, if necessary, for therapeutic purposes: in the breaking down of his defences and a regressive re-living of his experiences. In such a case he would need a high degree of

dependence on someone. In fact I was able to use the mother, who in spite of giving a neurotic impression proved herself to be able to act as Patrick's mental nurse. The good dream: "Bliss, to be cared for; I know I want this" was the indication which I later used as a pointer for management. I had nothing to tell me at this stage whether the mother could or could not meet his need (to be cared for); in fact, it seemed that she might be the worst person rather than the best.

Patrick returned to boarding school.

The next event was an emergency call from the mother and from Patrick: Would I see him immediately? Patrick had run away from school, and had taken the train home laden with Latin books. He said he had to get home to work at Latin, since he was not able to work at school and he was letting the school down. He had made a terrific effort to learn Latin all the way in the train, and at home he retired to bed to continue the intellectual effort. It will be noted that he was completely unable to ask for help on account of the threat of mental breakdown.

Second interview with Patrick
(two weeks after the first)

This was a comparatively uneventful interview. Patrick said that he had thought of running away in the autumn term. The thing was that a boy had made an elementary mistake and a master had said of this boy that he was fit to be caned and that he was not fit to be in the school. Patrick had reacted strongly to this minor incident. He had made himself sick, and had gone to the sickroom. Generally he displayed a paranoid disposition with hypersensitivity to any idea of punishment or censure. His housemaster, ordinarily a benign figure in his life, had become a threat.

Clinically Patrick had become a psychiatrically ill person, with no insight, and with paranoid-type anxieties.

After a quarter of an hour he dropped the rationalization that it was fear of failure in Latin that had brought him, and he said openly that it was the first interview and what he got from it that had brought him back, *though he had not known this till he actually came to see me.* He described how the faint word of disapproval on the part of the schoolmaster linked up with hallucinated voices. He did not fear being actually punished, because being punished was kept separate in his mind from the hallucinated voices.

I advised that he should stay at home over the week-end, and arranged this with the school. The staff told me they considered Patrick's mother was *too disturbed to be good for him,* but I insisted that he should stay at home.

Third interview with Patrick
(four days later)

On a Sunday Patrick was due to go back to school. He locked himself in the bathroom and would not come out, and would not see me. He was coaxed out and brought to see me as an emergency. I had to lure him out of his brother's sports car.

This third interview was a very intense one, and I was not able to take notes. It was a communication in a deeper layer, in which Patrick told me a great deal about himself and his family, and at the end I said: "You are not going back to school, but you are going to your cottage on the island. *You are ill.* As long as you are ill you can stay with your mother, and I will tell your mother what to do. And I will deal with the school for you." The important thing was that I told him he was ill.

He made a last effort to protest, remembering all he had looked forward to in the summer term at school, especially painting, and then with a sigh of relief he accepted what I said.

Comment: He was now *officially ill.* This was the crucial moment in the management of the case. It could be said from this moment he started on a slow process of recovery. But the first jump forward clinically came after the next interview in which the unknown factor of the first interview became elucidated.

The school was helpful though sceptical. The headmaster came to London and visited Patrick, and it was arranged that Patrick could go back to the school when well again, and without being hurried or harried.

Fourth interview with Patrick
(three days later)

Patrick came alone. He said that he had come for a specific reason, which was that he now understood the bouncing baby drawing (no. 12).

Trying to get at the meaning of this unexpected drawing, he had been talking things over with his mother and she had told him the story of his behaviour at one and a half years when she had had to go away for "six weeks" for an operation. While his mother was away he had stayed with friends who were supposed to be suitable, but they got him more and more excited. His father visited every day. In this period Patrick had become overexcitable, seeming happy, and always laughing and jumping up and down. He said: "It was like the drawing, and when mother told me about it all I remembered the bars of the cot." When his mother came back from the hospital (he went on to tell me) he saw her in her car, and suddenly all the bounce went, and he got on to her lap and went straight to sleep. It is said that he slept for twenty-four hours, and that his mother had kept him with her all that time. (This was the mother's first experience of the mental nursing of Patrick, and she was just about to have a second.)

Patrick had been describing to me a real incident, the feeling of which he had remembered. It was a period of danger at one and a half years, of a crescendo of manic defence, which quickly turned into a depression at the mother's return. Evidently there had been a real danger at this time of a snapping of the thread of the continuity of his being. The mother had come back only just in time, and she knew she must let him sleep on her lap till he should wake.

Patrick told me all this with deep feeling, and went on to say: "You see, I have never been able to be quite sure of mother since, and this had made me stick to her; and this meant I kept her from father; and I had not much use for father myself."

In all this Patrick was describing the illness which *antedated* the tragedy in which the father died. Patrick felt at this stage that he had manoeuvred the whole episode, which of course might have ended happily, but which in fact ended in disaster. He said he really had expected his mother to be pleased when his father died, and the mother's unexpected grief had simply made him confused. He had not been able to react to the actual drowning episode (except for the psychosomatic disorders at school) until the first interview with me, that is, eight months after the tragedy.

Patrick went away from this interview *immensely relieved*, and his mother reported a marked clinical improvement which persisted and gradually led on to his recovery.

Patrick now became able to criticize his mother without losing his love for her. In his words: "Two days of her, fine! Two plus, ghastly!"

Incidentally, describing an art exhibition that he went to with a friend, he said: "Pictures and painting, that's why I'm alive." He could now tell me: "Depression means that the world comes to an end."

Regression as a feature in the clinical state

There now started up an indefinite period of regression. He turned into a boy of 4, going everywhere with his mother and holding her hand. Nobody knew how long this would last. Much of the time Patrick spent in the holiday cottage. There a stray cat conveniently had four kittens. Patrick seemed to be completely identified with this mother cat. Eventually he brought the kittens to London for me to see them and opened the zip-fastener of his bag in my room, whereupon four kittens jumped out and went all over the house.

The mother telephoned (three weeks later) to let me know she had had a letter handed to her, written by Patrick in a very childish hand, it said:

1.   Do you love me?
2.   Thank you very much.
3.   Can I see Dr D.W.W. soon?

So a new visit was arranged for the next day.

Fifth interview with Patrick

Patrick had had a dream, and he had been frightened the whole
day. This dream was dreamed for the interview, and it is interesting that he knew he was liable to have this dream, so that he asked
for the interview several days before he dreamed it. It was a long
dream (no. 15), some of which I was able to take down.

THE DREAM

There was a church and the church had an altar (cf. previous
dream of church with no altar). There were three boxes and it
was generally understood that there were corpses in them. It
was thought that the far one on the left was most likely to turn
into a ghost, but actually it was the near one that became a
ghost. It showed some signs of life and sat up. It had a waxy
face and looked as if it had been drowned. Curiously enough
this ghost was female. It was a girl, and in describing the girl
he used the word "pristine." (It is rather characteristic of him
to use a word like that.) He said it was ominous.

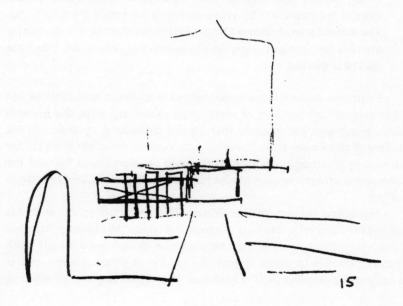

15

Some of the analysis of this dream was done in the course of the analysis of other dreams. In the end it turned out that he felt that this ghost was the ghost of his father, but of the female aspect of his father. He now said that the quarrels between his father and mother were between his mother's masculine self and his father's female self. In fact, as he said, he has not entirely lost a father because a father is still present in the mother.

> The dream went on in rather a long-winded way. Roughly speaking, this concerned a woman and a school in the island. They arrived there with a school friend. There was something about the tradition in the service in the chapel. This is why the boxes were in front of the altar. The seniors knew what was in the boxes. Patrick was told to go up to the altar and he suddenly knew that there were dead people in the boxes. After this there were two other episodes, each of which involved water. They went to watch a cricket match. There was something grey about it. He saw the school was going to collapse because of erosion by water, so 300 boys were drowned. Then his mother and the woman were with two boys. Water was rising higher and higher and lapping at the houses which started to crumble. The water covered his brother's sports car. The school friend seemed to get lost in the course of this, but he and his mother got away in the sports car, which by this time had reappeared.

From the associations spontaneously given it was clear about this dream that the fear of water was joined up with the general crumbling away of morale during the drowning episode. *In the telling of this dream Patrick reached very close to the actual agony of the drowning situation*, although in the first session when he told me about the drowning episode he had not been able to reach to deep affect.

He asked me two other things. The first had to do with his grandmother, who has had a stroke. He said: "Will you please tell me how either to alter her so that she is not so difficult with mother or else to make it possible for me to stand it when she is really quite impossible?" I told him that I had no way of altering either of these two things at all. There was nothing to do but to survive the awfulness of the relationship, particularly that existing between his mother and the grandmother, a relationship which had a history going right back to mother's early days and which, as Patrick said, very much accounted for mother's personal difficulties.

The other question had to do with Patrick's experiences during the last week of holiday. A boy with whom he had been camping provokingly pulled down the guy ropes: Patrick said: "All right, I'm going off" and the boy said: "I never did want you, *and my father never did want you either.*" This was very disturbing. He said he felt that other boys would be able to deal with this sort of thing in a friend, but for him his friend's behaviour produced a crisis. When his mother collected him in the car he broke down into crying. He emphasized that he felt that he ought not to be as upset as all this about such an incident. He gave all this as an example of the way he becomes upset and this joins up with the reaction to the criticism of another boy by the Latin master before he ran away from school. (If people are not friendly, then they quickly become associated in his mind with the latent paranoid potential.)

Comment: Patrick had now had time to get into touch with his guilt feelings and with the full agony of the crumbling morale, when he watched his father drown and when he himself nearly drowned too, but was rescued.

In dreaming this dream he showed that he had gained control over the episode, and in remembering and reporting it he had further displayed the strength of his ego-organization; also in arranging to see me he had shown his capacity to believe in his mother, and in me as a father substitute, and in our working together as parent figures acting in unison.

Sixth interview with Patrick
(nine days later)

Patrick used this interview to go into details about his depression that was related to his mother's absences. This was related in a complex way to the demands made on his mother by her own mother. He also told me that the threat of depression had always been with him, at least since the episode at the age of one and a half.

First interview with the mother
(a month later, five months after the initial telephone
conversation)

This was the first personal interview I had with the mother. The main reason why I had not seen her was that the case had come my way when I had no vacancy whatever, and I had to be economical in my use of my own time. The following account is built up from notes made during the interview. At this time Patrick had regressed to a state of dependence and immaturity, in the care of herself and the people in the locality. Here the mother's basic reliability had shown up.

The mother first of all talked about her relationship with her own mother, whose old age exaggerated her usual demanding nature. She went on to speak about Patrick and his anxieties about work and school. It appears that during his period of regression he got permission to go to a local school when he felt like it. Then Patrick found a blind man teacher.

I insisted, and in doing so supported the mother in her own ideas, that whatever was done in the way of education at this stage had to be done only if Patrick really wanted it, and no tests whatever were to be allowed. The mother described how sensitive Patrick could be:

"One sarcastic word annihilates him. He easily feels the ground cut from under his feet." I explained that her job was to wait for spontaneous forward movement and in no way to expect anything of Patrick at this stage. The mother said that Patrick already understood that he was getting better, and he had said it in these words: "If I were still ill Dr W. would see me immediately, wouldn't he!" This was in reaction to my having to make him wait for an appointment, the first time that I made him wait since he had come under my care. I took great trouble during this consultation to support the mother's intuition, or what she called her "instincts," especially as she felt the lack of the support that she used to get from her husband in her management of the children. Already Patrick had begun to think about his position in the school on his return and to worry about the possibility of having to stay down in a lower class for a year while his friends would move up. (A great deal was said during this consultation which was important from the point of view of the mother but which could not be noted at the time.)

Seventh interview with Patrick (a few days later)

Soon after this consultation a complication arose due to the school's failure to believe in Patrick's illness: examination papers arrived from the school and the result was almost a disaster. Patrick painfully gathered himself together out of his withdrawn state and attempted to meet the challenge. At the same time he lost all his capacity for relaxation and became seriously anxious and "persecuted." For the time being he emerged from his regressed and dependent state.

I arranged to see Patrick immediately and told him that I *absolutely prohibited* all tests and examinations, and that he should throw the papers away. Actually I said: "Put them in the lavatory and pull the plug," which was suitable in the circumstances, but when reported to the mother these words seemed to her to be dangerous. The mother had a parent's anxieties about school authorities, and she was afraid lest I had put these words in my letter to the headmaster. My perhaps clumsy interference in regard to the examination papers caused consternation in the school, and in any case it was not understandable to the headmaster and the housemaster, or to the school doctor, that this boy should be away from school leading a carefree life in the charge of his "neurotic" mother, without any father figure in his life, and completely neglecting his education. Yet this was exactly what he needed.

The immediate result of this consultation and of my making the decision about the test papers in a firm way was that Patrick regained his relaxed manner and returned quickly to a withdrawn

and regressed state and became once more completely happy in
the country cottage. In this way he did quite a lot of work with the
examination papers without anxiety, and he called this "playing
with them."

The first anniversary of the drowning episode

It was important that the mother asked me to discuss with her by
telephone the arrangements for the first anniversary. There had
been a tendency to arrange for a sort of party, with a lot of people
coming in, and the sort of feverish activity which would cover up
the wound. This would have been a new version of the bouncing
baby episode. With my help the mother and Patrick arranged to be
alone together on the afternoon of this the first anniversary of the
tragedy, which was also, of course, Patrick's birthday.

Afterward the mother described what happened. She said that
Patrick looked excessively tired, and indeed they were both worn
out. They sat together all the afternoon and heard the clock tick by.
Thus the time passed. Then Patrick said: "Oh thank goodness
that's over, it wasn't half as bad as I thought it was going to be."
Immediately he seemed a much more healthy boy. His face "came
undone." It could be said that the regression and withdrawn state
changed at this point into a progression, a movement forward
towards independence and participation.

Eighth interview with Patrick
(six months after the initial contact)

Patrick came and reported a dream he had had. He was talking
with Sir X (a well-known writer and art critic and a friend of the
family). There was emphasis on the word Sir. He was very nice.
The "Sir" probably related this father figure to the idea of his
housemaster. In this way Patrick was reporting to me the return of
live father figures in his inner psychic reality. There was a good
deal more in what Patrick talked about which had to do with men,
and also about his older brother.

Ninth interview with Patrick
(two months later, a year and a half after the drowning episode)

This was more or less a social event in which we talked about a wide range of matters and Patrick drew a skyscraper which he called "Sunset over Rio" (no. 16).

Letter to school

Before this ninth interview I wrote to the school recommending Patrick's return, and I included in the letter the following paragraph:

> I want to emphasize that I do feel that Patrick has had quite a serious breakdown. I would say that he has now recovered and that probably he is in a better state than he was in before his father's death. Certain symptoms of early childhood have disappeared. There is a residual symptom which may give a little trouble and that has to do with his extreme sensitivity in regard to praise and blame. It may help those who are work-

16

ing with him to know that it is not the big things that worry Patrick; he is not really disturbed if somebody is very angry with him, because this is real and is related to the actual situation objectively perceived. What so easily upsets Patrick is just a very little blame or praise and the effect of these two can be quite out of proportion to anything real. I think he knows about this and will try to stop himself from excessive reactions. If you have to be openly angry with Patrick, then this is not the sort of thing that I believe will cause trouble.

From the point of view of the school Patrick was in a satisfactory state. The staff soon forgot that he had been ill and probably found it difficult to believe that Patrick had in fact had a serious breakdown.

Second interview with the mother
(after the last interview with Patrick)

This second interview with the mother was important, and was necessary because of the mother's anger with me, which needed to find expression. In the course of the interview it emerged that I had put a very big strain on her, and indeed I knew I had done this. I had in fact asked her to *postpone her own reaction to her husband's death* in order to nurse Patrick, and I had relied on her to take responsibility for him during his breakdown. Moreover, there were many ways, some undoubtedly reasonable, in which Patrick's mother found herself annoyed with me. I had left her "out on a limb." After thoroughly expressing her dissatisfaction with me and letting me know that the school was also angry with me she became very friendly and grateful. She then told me how helping Patrick had helped her herself.

Third interview with the mother
(a week later)

I was able to check up with the mother on the details of her leaving Patrick when he was one and a half years old. It was *after* my first long interview with Patrick that she told Patrick about this. While she was telling him he became intensely interested and said: "I remember hitting a cot." The reason why the mother told him this story was that after the first consultation with me, when Patrick was very much changed by his contact with me, she began to think back.

She talked to a woman friend who told her that the place where Patrick had been sent when she went away from him at one and a half years was not a good place, and that she had known this at the time. She added: "It was a family in which everyone is pepped up, and children are trained vigorously." Recounting these details made the mother think of a still earlier incident. At five days Patrick was hospitalized for six weeks on account of vomiting, and his weight went down from 9 pounds to 6 pounds. At six weeks the mother took him home, whereupon "he put on weight like a bomb."

Fourth interview with the mother
(six months later, two years after the husband's death)

The mother reported that Patrick had made good progress. He was top of his form at school (not a high form) and he was enjoying work; the school report was good. She said he was happier and sleeping well and his phobias, which he had had at home since he was a little boy, had dwindled to nothing. He had enjoyed his holidays, being always occupied in his own way, and he had stayed with a school friend in the cottage, which he got ready for his mother.

His insight is shown by the plans that he was making for the second anniversary of the tragedy. He found that he had arranged to go with friends to another island! When he realized the date for which this expedition had been planned, he said: "Not that day. No. It would not be good to be by the sea then." So he cancelled this holiday to which he had been looking forward. There was no wish to bypass the tragic moment. He was still not quite at ease when near the sea and he made the comment: "Fancy it's nearly two years," implying that he was still very near to the feeling belonging to the tragedy. The mother was helping him to plan a very simple day for the second anniversary.

Reconstruction of Patrick's illness

1. Unknown effect of the hospitalization at five days to six weeks with sudden clinical improvement dating from the moment of the baby's return home.

2. The dangerous separation from the mother at one and a half years. The family in which he was placed encouraged a manic defence, but on the return of the mother there was sudden recovery in the form of depression, which was clinically hidden in the twenty-four-hour sleep on her lap.

3. Following this there was a bond between the boy and the mother which had behind it not only love but also his uncertainty about her reliability. *Here was a relative deprivation.* This made Patrick somewhat mother-bound and it interfered with the development of his relationship to his father.

4. The development of Patrick's personality during the latency period was distorted and, as the mother put it, it seemed as if he was destined to become mother-fixated.

5. Then came the tragedy which, though partly accidental, was felt by Patrick to be engineered by his unconscious processes.

6. Next followed the delay in the development of Patrick's reaction to the tragedy. He seemed unaffected and went back to boarding school. Here, however, he tended to go to the sickroom for obscure disorders. He engineered these, but without knowing why.

7. The first interview with me. This was brought about by the mother, who began to sense that Patrick was becoming oversensitive and liable to psycho-somatic disorder. Here was a paranoid clinical state of increasing severity. The mother also knew that Patrick had not reacted to the tragedy. In this interview Patrick took the trouble to make me understand that *his difficulties started a long time before the tragedy.* He drew a picture which in a later interview gave the clue to the original trauma.

8. Truancy from school for a subsidiary reason. In the second interview Patrick knew that he had come to me for help, and that he was threatened with a mental breakdown. A regressive withdrawal state could appear instead of the paranoid illness

because of the fact of his belief in me, which had been engendered in the first interview.

9. *My decision that he was ill,* and that he must not go back to school for an indefinite period. This quickly led to his reaching a deep level of regression to dependence and to his becoming withdrawn. The mother met this dependence more than adequately. To do this she had to postpone her own reaction to the loss of her husband.

10. The arrival of feelings appropriate to the tragedy (fifth interview). At the depth of his breakdown Patrick brought the dream, which led to his experiencing the affect that had been experienced neither at the time of the traumatic episode nor subsequently. After the experiencing of these feelings Patrick began to lose his need to be ill. He began to recover.

11. Return to boarding school. He was now nearly well and had not lost much ground in schoolwork. He entered his old form for another year and accepted the situation. He quickly resumed emotional growth appropriate to his age.

Final comment

Patrick had a delayed reaction to a tragedy in which he was involved at the age of 11 years. The delay belonged partly to the fact that he was already ill at the time of the tragedy, and the tragic episode could be said to be a part of the boy's total illness. This illness had as an aetiological factor a dangerous period of separation from the mother at one and a half years. (Possibly, a pattern for his reaction to this illness was set up by his earliest illness and separation from five days to six weeks at the beginning of his life.) The acute illness, for the management of which I was responsible, started with the tragedy and the delayed reaction, and this illness can now be said to be at an end.[4] The total result is that Patrick has lost the major part of the illness from which he suffered *before* the

---

[4]Follow-up: Four years after the tragedy the boy's development can be said to be natural and healthy.—*D.W.W.*

tragedy, which was of the nature of a deprivation reaction, and which was characterized by a degree of mother-fixation, by a schizoid distortion in his reality testing (phobic system), by a tendency to deny depression, and a personality disturbance leading towards homosexuality with a paranoid colouring.

The main therapeutic provision was the way in which the boy's mother met his regression to dependence, and along with this there was specific help given by myself on demand.

CHAPTER TWO

On holding as metaphor: Winnicott and the figure of St Christopher

John Forrester

W innicott is not famous for his writings on fathers. On mothers, yes; on children and mothers, yes; and on the holding environment, very much so. It is therefore interesting to reflect on a case in which the father's fate and the analyst's position in relation to that father were paramount. Such was described in Winnicott's paper, "A Child Psychiatry Case Illustrating Delayed Reaction to Loss", which opens: "On his eleventh birthday Patrick suffered the loss of his father by drowning."

My commentary is devoted to Winnicott's management of Patrick's treatment, but also to how Winnicott negotiates the

This chapter was originally delivered as the Madeleine Davis Memorial Lecture on 14 May 1995. It was Madeleine who brought Winnicott's paper on delayed reaction to loss to my attention, when she and I were both members of a psychoanalytic reading group in Cambridge at the beginning of the 1980s. Its reading, and Madeleine's comments upon it, had a profound effect on my view of Winnicott and indeed of psychoanalytic practice in general. This chapter is dedicated to her memory.

themes latent in the traumatic scene in which the father drowned. Patrick lost his father; his father lost his life. It is the connection between these two losses that had to be managed in the treatment. And, to delve a little more deeply into the Winnicottian themes evoked by this treatment, I shall turn to fictional and political versions of this traumatic scene: the father who holds a child above the water, who shelters the child in the wind and the rain, who protects the child at all costs. Even at the cost of his life.

Patrick's mother had telephoned Winnicott on the advice of a friend. "I was told that the father had been drowned in a sailing accident, that Patrick had been to some extent responsible for the tragedy, and that she, the mother, and the older son, were still very disturbed and that the effect on Patrick had been complex." The mother felt that Patrick's state was delicate and decided to risk having someone investigate, despite being deeply suspicious of anything smelling of psychotherapy.

Winnicott saw the boy a total of nine times in the course of a little over a year, starting two months after the first telephone conversation, which was already some months after the tragedy. He also saw the mother four times. The paper is, to my mind, an exemplary presentation of a number of distinctively Winnicottian themes: about how loss, and more specifically loss of continuity, is dealt with—and also about how to go about conceiving of the linkage between losses at different times of life. The paper is also an illustration—this is a word Winnicott was very fond of using when talking of cases: "one case proves nothing, but it may illustrate much" (1968a, p. 369)—of how to manage a case without psychotherapeutic intervention of any extensive sort. Managing such a case involves making an assessment of the patient but also, equally importantly, of what Winnicott called his environment: in this instance, the boy's mother. So the case was actually not treated, but only managed by Winnicott, often by letter and by telephone, by his keeping in place a holding environment. It is his method of managing by keeping something in place and thereby maintaining a role with an essential connection to the father's function. Winnicott's interventions evince—inevitably, it might be said, given the little time and space that Winnicott had to work in and with—a minimalism that is totally in tune with the demands of repetition and regression that the traumatic scene required. But this minimalism is not a quietism or inertia—far from it. Winnicott's actions are absolutely crucial to the resolution of the case precisely because he acted with such decisiveness. Managing cases in this manner, his example indicates, is only for those with their feet firmly planted on the ground.

The management started with him provoking—if that is not too strong a word—a nervous breakdown in the boy.

> A regressive withdrawal state could appear instead of the paranoid illness because of the fact of his belief in me, which had been engendered in the first interview. . . . *My decision that he was ill*, and that he must not go back to school for an indefinite period. This quickly led to his reaching a deep level of regression to dependence and to his becoming withdrawn.

The means he employed are the ones any reader of Winnicott's is familiar with: he played the Squiggle game with him. If anything demonstrates that playing the Squiggle game with a child is a dangerous business, this paper does; I am reminded of the Minister of Transport who warned drivers that when they go out driving they should be careful because they have in their hands a weapon as dangerous as a loaded gun. It is strange to think of a crayon in Winnicott's hand as a dangerous weapon, but power comes in strange and mysterious forms.

Once the breakdown had been provoked, some two weeks after the initial interview, Winnicott's skills as a manager came into play; he used his authority as a highly reputable member of the medical profession to fend off Patrick's boarding school, who could not believe that Patrick was really ill, since they did not know—or, more plausibly, it had never occurred to them, and, if it had, they would not have believed it—that one interview with a psychiatrist could provoke a genuine nervous breakdown in a boy. Patrick's breakdown had landed him back at home, and the school agreed to Winnicott's advice that there he should stay for the indefinite future. Whenever the school wished to know how long "indefinite was", Winnicott would reassert his authority by conducting a "holding operation". Delaying, prevaricating, putting them off—this is how Winnicott's actions probably appeared to them. In reality, all his actions were the opposite of procrastination, "the thief of time": all were decisive and aimed at *gaining time* for Patrick. I am reminded of Winnicott's response to the question that analysts have to answer for themselves: when is the best moment to offer the patient an interpretation? Winnicott's response to the question was: "I think that it is the earliest possible moment that is the right moment for an interpretation, that is to say *the earliest moment at which the material makes it clear what to interpret*. But I am economical in my interpretations, and if I am not sure what to interpret I have no hesitation in playing for time" (1958a, p. 122). This delightfully paradoxical formulation—he did not hesitate to play for time—captures well the decisiveness with which one must act if one is not to be trapped into time that is waiting-time rather than play-time. Winnicott acted decisively to "hold off" the school so as to secure this play-time for Patrick.

He also persuaded the mother to postpone her own mourning for her husband and occupy herself with her son; this "mental nursing", as Winnicott called it, was to his mind the principal agent of Patrick's eventual cure. Winnicott paid in the end for the renunciation he asked of the mother: when Patrick's treatment— her mental nursing of him—was effectively completed and Patrick had returned to his boarding school, she expressed considerable annoyance with Winnicott for having, as she put it, left her "out on a limb". It was Winnicott who put this phrase in quotation marks, in order to underline the fact that she had accused him, in effect, of not holding her adequately; as if, in the course of their telephone conversations, he had died, leaving her talking into thin air. Like her husband, you might say. It was almost as if Winnicott made a quick calculation: both need help, but it is the boy who needs help far more, and the mother will just have to shoulder the burden of Patrick's cure. It is either her or him. And Winnicott made it difficult for the mother to refuse to sacrifice herself for her son and thus repeat her husband's action. Winnicott highlighted for himself and for the reader the fact that the mother might also have been aware of the metaphoric resonances of the holding cure that Winnicott asked her to conduct; the only words from her that he quoted directly in his report of the first interview with her were the following: "One sarcastic word annihilates him. He easily feels the ground cut from under his feet."

In what I have said so far I have been implicitly moving towards a specifically temporal interpretation of the act of holding.

When one holds something, one holds it spatially above. Despite this spatial meaning being essential, there is no holding without a temporal dimension: you must hold something *for a certain amount of time* for it to count as holding (think of the rules governing catches in ball games). Winnicott attached sufficient importance to this temporal aspect to name the exact period of time of holding: twenty-four hours. But this time of holding is very rarely time devoted to holding and nothing else. One does not hold a child simply in order to hold it, any more than one holds a pen or a football whistle just in order to hold it. In addition, children notoriously cannot sit still; just as well known is the fact that a woman's work is never done, and the parent who spends most of his or her day holding a child immobile would be a strange parent indeed. When one holds a child, one *moves*, one is *active*, one is *going somewhere*. This may not necessarily be physical locomotion; it may be the activity of imaginative movement, of play. But one should bear in mind that the holding activity is both spatial—holding above—and temporal—holding over a period of time. The holding environment is, in effect, a fused spatio-temporal container. Winnicott was very attentive to these limits, as his dicta concerning psychoanalytic technique make clear.

I have been proceeding gradually towards the tragedy and Patrick's story in part because I want, without duplicating it, to communicate something of Winnicott's own narrative strategy. He writes in the opening paragraphs of his paper:

> Whenever possible I get at the history of a case by means of psychotherapeutic interviews *with the child*. The history gathered in this way contains the vital elements, and it is of no matter if in certain respects the history taken in this way proves to be incorrect. The history taken in this way evolves itself, according to the child's capacity to tolerate the facts.

He proceeds in this way with Patrick, learning in the first interview of Patrick's version of the tragedy in the water when Patrick's father lost his life. Then, unlike other psychoanalytic accounts of a traumatic incident of this sort, the rest of the paper does not really tell us anything more about the tragedy. We are left to wonder about its contradictions and its significance for Patrick's inner life. What "really" happened? This is one of the questions that has acquired political urgency in today's psychotherapeutic climate. For Winnicott, it is not a pressing question, in large part because he makes as if he is managing the case, not engaging in psychotherapy. Instead of analysing the significance of this life-and-death tragedy, Winnicott's principal interpretation in the whole case came in the third interview, shortly after Patrick's breakdown:

> "You are not going back to school, but you are going to your cottage on the island. *You are ill.* As long as you are ill you can stay with your mother, and I will tell your mother what to do. And I will deal with the school for you." The important thing was that I told him he was ill.

It may seem strange to call this an interpretation. However, Winnicott's own writing here underlines this view; he places the words "you are ill" in italics.

There is a whole essay to be written about Winnicott's use of italics. At the end of this paper, in his concluding remarks, Winnicott once again italicized this moment—which he called *"My decision that he was ill"*—as the crucial intervention. We can compare this intervention with another paper about a consultation with a young patient, an adolescent girl, where he writes:

> I had an interview with G. herself, and as result of this and a general survey of the whole problem I decided to come down heavily on the side of a diagnosis of *health* complicated by emotional and physical disturbances that belong to a certain kind of development. [Winnicott, 1968a, p. 370]

In this passage the word "health" is in italics—it is the only italicized word in the whole paper.

With Patrick, the decision that he was ill, and Winnicott's decision to build his communication with Patrick around telling him that this was so, orients us away from psychotherapy towards medical management. It is, of course, also in line with Winnicott's view that there are always forces of development and self-cure operating in patients, if only the environment can be organized in a way that gives them the freedom and space to act. Having established trust with Patrick in the first interview, which provoked his breakdown, Winnicott now told Patrick that he was ill, which provoked an indefinite regression. A few weeks later, in the fifth interview, Patrick brought an important dream, in which the element of his fear of water allowed him to reach *"very close to the actual agony of the drowning situation"*—which, it should be noted, Winnicott said "had been experienced neither at the time of the traumatic incident nor subsequently". With this dream, Patrick began "to lose his need to be ill. He began to recover".

Winnicott's decision that Patrick was ill, and his decision to tell him this and to make it clear that this was the most important thing he had to tell him, placed Patrick's treatment firmly in the medical dimension. I remain deeply impressed by the virtuosity of Winnicott's action here: to use a medical decision as a way of communicating the principal psychoanalytic interpretation in the case. By which I mean that Winnicott communicated to Patrick that he was ill, that is, not dead, but living and needing to recover; also, and crucially, that he was not identified with the dead father in the water. And, beyond this speculative reading of Winnicott's interpretative strategy, there is another way of seeing what Winnicott was doing: think of the importance that Winnicott attached in so many of his writings to clarity about the proper way to conduct a medical practice. When I read these writings of Winnicott's on medicine and case work, I cannot but link them to Michael Balint's work of the same period with general practitioners to establish the appropriate environment and ethos of the medical system created by the National Health Service. Winnicott on management and the holding company, Balint on the GP and the joint stock investment company: these are key psycho-political metaphors of British medicine and the Welfare State in the period after the Second World War. Telling Patrick he was ill was the keystone of the management of the case; it was the equivalent of telling the school, as he had done, that he *"absolutely prohibited* all tests and examinations"—again those italics strike one's eye: the words *ABSOLUTELY PROHIBITED*, which are as strong as language ever gets, are in italics.

A position of absolute prohibition, of decisive decisions, is an attribute of the father that Patrick had lost. Or, to put it in a Lacanian dialect, a voice with such authority is that of the symbolic, as opposed to the imaginary, father. Winnicott could not but be sensitive to the question of his taking on the position of father; he notes how he took great trouble to support the mother's intuition, "especially as she felt the lack of support she used to get from her husband in her management of the children". But his allusions to the paternal function that he took on are all of this sort: he assimilates the function of the symbolic father to the management of the mother, of the family, of the school. It is the father who holds by managing.

But what of the other father, the father who sailed a boat that sank and who was with Patrick in the water till he sank and drowned, leaving Patrick alone in the water as night came on? Is this not the archetypal situation of not being held? Is this not the Winnicottian nightmare *par excellence*? And surely the details of the incident are important here? What are we to make of the fact that the boy had a life-jacket and the father did not? One way of shocking ourselves into thinking about this is to imagine the father deciding to take the life-jacket from his son, letting his son drown, and thereby perhaps—and only perhaps—saving his own life. Why did the father not do this? And what was the effect on Patrick of him not doing that? Is that what Patrick was thinking of when he said to Winnicott: "After a long time in the water one began to fight for oneself"? Or did this comment imply that Patrick was, in effect, prepared to fight for himself, to re-enact the Hegelian dialectic of master and slave: either him or me, in a struggle to death. With his own father.

But the father was not prepared to fight to the death: he preferred to drown, rather than live at the cost of his son's life. What did Patrick make of that fact? Did the father who let himself drown symbolize the father who held his son, in the very act of drowning? Would there have been a place here for that paradoxical interpretation so characteristic of the analysis of the transference, which we find in Patrick Casement's well-known paper, "Some Pressures on the Analyst for Physical Contact during the Reliving of an Early Trauma" (1982). In that paper, Casement *not* holding his patient's hand meant precisely the same as his holding her hand *symbolically*. Did Patrick's father hold his son by not holding him, by drowning instead? Or was the father who abandoned his son and preferred death—Patrick thought that his mother or his father would have committed suicide anyway—the epitome of the parent who drops the child?

Winnicott passed by all these questions. But, having emphasized that he behaved like a doctor engaged in managing the cure, the care-cure, note how Winnicott then behaved like a psychoanalyst, by seeking the dynamic of the care-cure not in the "actual agony" of the drowning situation, but further back in time—in another trauma. But he did not do what one also expects the psychoanalyst to do: address questions of transference or countertransference. Imagine the transference based on this scene of drowning: either a transferential re-enactment that would be a dialectic of live father and dead son (the neurotic transference), or dead father and live son (the psychotic transference, in which it is the psychoanalyst's failings, his failure to hold, that prove curative). Remember what Winnicott said about analysis with patients whose environments failed them in early childhood:

> The patient now hates the analyst for the failure that originally came as an environmental factor, outside the infant's omnipotent control, but that is *now* staged in the transference. So in the end we succeed by failing—failing the patient's way. ... [My patient] *will make me fail* in ways determined by her past history. [Winnicott, 1963b, pp. 258-259]

Winnicott avoided this infernal transference with Patrick, in large part by leap-frogging to the earlier trauma that, Patrick had made clear to him, had made him ill long before the drowning of his father.

Two elements led Winnicott to the earlier trauma. One was a picture that Patrick drew for Winnicott in the first interview: a picture of a dream that he had of a baby jumping up and down, screaming. Winnicott inferred that it was a picture of Patrick at 18 months, the age Patrick gave to the baby. About a month after drawing this picture, Patrick arranged a special session with Winnicott, the fourth interview, deliberately to tell him the meaning of this picture and the dream. When he was 18 months old, his mother was away from him for six weeks having an operation and had left him with a rowdy family who over-excited him. When she came back to her over-excited baby, Patrick felt all his bounce go out of him and climbed onto her lap and went to sleep. He slept for twenty-four hours, his mother with him the whole time.

In Winnicott's account, we are never allowed to know which was the traumatic loss referred to in the title of his paper—Patrick's mother's absence at 18 months or his father's death at 11 years. In this, he is entirely true to the structure of psychoanalytic explanation as laid down by Freud in his *Project for a Scientific Psychology* (1895) and in the seduction theory: it takes two events, separated by an indefinite, timeless period of time, to make a trauma. Like Freud in the Wolf Man case, Winnicott even adds in a third event, when mother remembers that, at the age of 5 days, Patrick was taken to hospital for six weeks on account of vomiting and lost weight disastrously. Only when the mother took him home again did "he put on weight like a bomb". So there are three losses: the loss of his father at 11 years, the loss of his mother at 18 months, and the loss of the breast at 5 days. Is this paper a contribution to the theory—the causal theory—of object loss and environmental failure? It is not clear. Winnicott is, as I have indicated, silent, perhaps playfully abstemious, in his exploration of the metaphorics of the traumatic scene in the water, when the father failed to hold his son—or held him so well that the son survived because of the renunciation of the father. Otherwise, we might have seen this paper become a contribution to the metaphorics of holding. Instead, with his elegance and habitual economy, Winnicott is primarily intent on letting his reader know how he manages a case like this one.

Yet I have felt that one cannot entirely avoid the drowning episode. It is imagining the agony in the water that haunts me. And I ask: how could Winnicott be so circumspect about one of the archetypal scenes of holding? It is at this point that I turn to a work that is in many respects the opposite of Winnicott's paper: instead of circumspection about the metaphorics of holding, this work analyses in innumerable variations the metaphorics of holding. It is, therefore, a work that helps one to think about Winnicott's overall vision of the relationship between the child and the environment, and also enables one to keep in focus the question of the father. The work in question is Michel Tournier's novel *Le Roi des Aulnes* (*The Erl King*), the central theme of which is a man whose life is dedicated to the ecstasy of carrying children.

The central character is Abel Tiffauges, a Frenchman, a huge, gentle man. The novel unfolds the destiny of his love of children, his paedophilia. In the opening scenes of the book, set just before the Second World War, while working as a car mechanic, he is arrested for molesting two young girls; the war intervenes, and, instead of prison, he finds himself first in the French army, then, with the capitulation of France, in a prisoner-of-war camp, from where he is moved to the heart of Nazi Germany, where, because of his peculiar charm and his ability to understand the mythical blood-hungry forces at work in that country, he is employed as a servant, first in Hermann Goering's hunting lodge and finally at a castle in Eastern Prussia, where the flower of Hitler's German Youth are prepared for the final martyrdom in the last days of the war.

The Erl King of the title of the book is the Erl King of Goethe's poem, which is also familiar in Schubert's magnificent setting. The poem depicts a father riding through a forest bearing in his arms his young son, who cries out to his father that the Erl King, the spirit of wind and forest, is tempting him to follow him. "Father can't you see the Erl King? . . . My son, it's the swirling of the mist." The father ignores his son's cries, pressing him closer to his chest and riding faster and faster. When he arrives home, his son is dead in his arms.

The Erl King is the pagan lover of children, who in the novel is equated with a prehistoric ancestor of all the Germans whose mummified body is dug up out of the stinking swamps. This Erl King is also Hitler, who every 20 April, on his birthday, receives, as if he were a new version of the Pied Piper, half a million German boys and a half a million German girls as a gift from his people, these children having been transformed by pagan rites of passage into Hitler's Children. Tiffauges—the French ogre, as he comes to be called and to see himself—comes originally from the Christian tradition; it is only subsequently that he recognizes the Nazi pagan mythology as one more version of his own. As in Melville's *Moby Dick*, everything in his life is a symbol, just like the insane Teutonic world of blood and death into which he has fallen. His early life, which we realize later was only a preparation for his destiny in the German war, was lived under the sign of St Christopher, the saint who carried Christ. His later life in Nazi

Germany is lived under the sign of the Erl King. The Erl King and Christopher; Hitler and Abel Tiffauges; German and French; pagan and Christian—all these are versions and perversions of Tiffauges' destiny, which is to love, to carry, to hold children.

How I see the theme of holding in Winnicott's work may be clarified by the version of the story of St Christopher that Tournier gives his hero early in the book. The story tells of a huge, ugly man who wishes to serve, but only a king who is more powerful than every other. Having found the service of a king with many subjects, he one day catches the king muttering strange incantations against the devil; perceiving that his master is afraid of this stronger authority, he seeks out the devil and pledges his service to him. But one day, his new master passes a cross on the wayside and shudders in distaste. His servant immediately goes in search of this new sovereign, who is even more powerful than the devil. A hermit tells him that Christ cannot be found so easily, and that he must fast. The man says that he is too big and strong to fast; there must be some other way to find this king. The hermit tells him to go and live in a house beside a nearby dangerous river and carry all travellers across it.

One day, the big man hears the voice of a child but cannot find the caller; at the third call, a frail young boy appears and asks to be taken across the river. The big man willingly takes him, but, as they cross, the child seems to increase in weight, till the man almost drowns. He does, however, reach the other side and asks the child how it is that he seems so slight and yet was so heavy. The child replies that he is the Christ, who is the world, and so his servant has just carried the world across the river. He tells the big man that if he does not believe him he should go back to his home, where there is new tree that has just burst into flower. Thereupon the child vanishes, the man returns home to find the flowering tree. And that is how the man got his name: Christopher, the Christ-carrier.

This Christopher is in search of an absolute Master and is prepared to sacrifice himself for that absolute Master. When first the king and then the devil expressed fear of someone more powerful than they, their servant realized that he was stronger than they were, because, like the figure of Siegfried in Wagner's *Ring*, fear of the stronger is the fundamental weakness of the weak.

Christopher spent his life in search of absolute strength; the Christ child taught him that he himself was the embodiment of absolute strength because he had been strong enough to carry the whole world—but only because he believed he was carrying a weak, defenceless, and almost invisible child, not realizing that he was the most powerful king in the world—a king powerful enough to bring forth at will a tree in blossom.

In the final section of *The Erl King*, the French ogre finds the fulfilment of his life, in preparing beautiful young boys for their death in battle. There is a scene where he experiences the quintessence of the ecstasy of carrying—*"l'extase phorique"* (Tournier, 1970, p. 365)—when he visits the death bier of one of his young charges, who had had his head blown off when the young boys were practising using anti-tank weapons, and picks up the boy's body. But, while the young Germans prepare to die, Tiffauges begins to withdraw from their rites. He encounters and rescues a young Jewish boy, escaped from Auschwitz, and carries him back on his horse through the misty German forests to the castle. He nurses the skeletal boy back to life. And the final scene of the book is of the French ogre carrying the young Jewish survivor on his shoulders into a boggy marsh as the apocalypse of the Russian invasion engulfs them both. As he moves deeper and deeper into the mud, the final sentence of the book reads: "When he raised his head towards Ephraim for the last time, all he saw was a golden six-pointed star turning slowly in the dark sky" (p. 393).

Tournier's novel is at one level a story of how the darkness of a sexual pervert in pre-war France is transformed by the circumstances of the political mythology of Nazism into something completely different: a white version of the Nazi ideal of the leader who carries his people to their deliverance. In France, Tiffauges can only be a sexual pervert. In Germany, he emerges as the benign mirror-image of Hitler, carrying children to their destinies. But, through the theme of carrying, the book is also a meditation on the very idea of metaphor. Metaphor is nothing other than the principal sexual activity of Tiffauges: "meta-phor" means precisely to carry across, just as Christopher means to carry Christ, the whole world, across. So Christopher is the ultimate metaphor for metaphor; he is metaphor made flesh. To carry across is to create meaning, and Tiffauges' life embodies and creates the meaning of the Nazi mythology. It thus reveals the possibility of perversion at the heart of the act of carrying across, of metaphor. And, by reading it beside Winnicott, we can see what becomes of holding when it is extended into the sphere of the erotic—it becomes paedophilia.

At the outset, Abel Tiffauges is perceived by his society as a sexual pervert—Tournier's prescience of our present distraction around paedophilia is striking. It is fair to say that paedophilia is the perversion of our age, the one that strikes most terror into our hearts, as we can gauge by our different reaction to, say, necrophilia, which is far less anxious. Perhaps it is the fact that the hero who holds is a man that links him to sexual perversion. Certainly, we used to think it less likely that a woman holding a small child is a paedophile. It is part of the shift away from classical psychoanalysis, a shift in significant part brought about by Winnicott, that we have become familiar, too familiar, with the image of mother as maternal holder and are startled by Freud's image of motherhood as a plenitude of eroticism:

> A mother's love for the infant she suckles and cares for is something far more profound than her later affection for the growing child. It is in the nature of a completely satisfying love-relation, which not only fulfils every mental wish but also every physical need; and if it represents one of the forms of attainable human happiness, that is in no little measure due to the possibility it offers of satisfying, without reproach, wishful impulses which have long been repressed and which must be called perverse. In the happiest marriage the father is aware that the baby, especially if he is a baby son, has become his rival, and this is the starting-point of an antagonism towards the favourite which is deeply rooted in the unconscious. [Freud, 1910, p. 115]

Tournier's novel restores the connection between the eroticism of carrying a child and the profound resonances of protectiveness and care, of the calm, maternal ecstasy of the burden. Turning back to Winnicott's work, we see that this carrying across is intimately linked with the metaphor of holding. The mother provides continuity in the baby's experience of the world, creates continuity. It is the breaking of continuity that means the baby feels dropped, which, as Adam Phillips recently pointed out (1995, p.

13), is the fundamental trauma for Winnicott. In Patrick's case, Winnicott described the six-week absence of the mother as giving rise to "a real danger at this time of a snapping of the thread of the continuity of his being", which was prevented only by the long sleep in her lap. This figure of the child asleep—or dead—in the mother's lap is a familiar one: we know it as the Pietà. The dead child on the mother's lap is another version of St Christopher—or vice versa. Everywhere Christ goes, it seems, there are images of children being held. It reminds me of an interesting exchange between Freud and Jung in 1910, when Freud tried to persuade Jung that "wood" was always a symbol for mother, because wood in Spanish is *madera*, also *matter*, and *mater* lies at the root of *materia*. The dying man on the wooden cross is another metaphor for Christopher's burden, his Pietà.

I shall finish with some remarks about politics. You may think that it is a long way from Patrick's ordeal in the water to the foundation of democracy. But it is precisely Winnicott's own thinking that I shall be following here, his thinking as stimulated by his passing over in silence the central trauma of not being held that Patrick experienced. I have emphasized—or offered a cogent speculation—that Winnicott's use of medical language of illness with Patrick was deliberate and strategic. Most clearly it went hand in hand with his notion of managing the case. Managing was, for him, the extension of holding. Psychotherapy, medicine, and social work were like concentric circles of holding, centred on the fundamental metaphor or experience of a child being held by its mother. Winnicott distinguished two sorts of medical activity, one of which is conducted by those who specialize "in cure to eradicate evil agencies". The other he called care-cure:

> . . . care-cure is an extension of the concept of holding. It starts with the baby in arms, and enrichment comes from the growth process in the infant, which the mother makes possible because of her knowing just what it is like to be this particular baby that she has given birth to.
>
> The theme of the facilitating environment enabling personal growth and the maturational process has to be a description of father–mother care, and of the family function, and this leads on to the whole build-up of democracy as a political extension of family facilitation, with the mature in-

dividual eventually taking part according to their age and capacity in politics and in the maintenance and rebuilding of the political structure. [Winnicott, 1970a, pp. 119–120]

Elsewhere he puts it as follows:

> . . . much of infant nurture is an ever-widening interpretation of the word "holding". Holding comes to include all physical management, in so far as it is done in adaptation to an infant's needs. Gradually a child values being let go, and this corresponds with the presentation to the child of the Reality Principle, which at first clashes with the Pleasure Principle (omnipotence abrogated). The family continues this holding, and society holds the family. [Winnicott, 1961, p. 107]

I want to suggest that this metaphor of holding has strong resonances within our specific post–Judaeo-Christian culture because of what Michel Foucault (1988) called the pastoral source of modern politics. Foucault pointed out that the notion of the individual is not to be found in the Greek ideal of the public space and the public citizen but, rather, stems from the Hebraic desert people's conception of the Shepherd God. The Shepherd God is another version of Christopher: he seeks out the defenceless and lost lamb and carries it back, in the wind and rain, to the safety of the flock. Foucault argues that it is this model of the Shepherd and the Flock that gives rise to all our modern closed institutions, with their fundamental recognition of the individual, originally the lost, the sinful individual; modernity is characterized by these closed institutions organized on the flock principle, stemming originally from the monastery, via the school, the asylum, and the military barracks, to the factory and the clinic. The modern conception of the family is also modelled on this essentially closed institution: a private space that holds the individuals within it. These closed spaces are to be contrasted with the open institutions of the market, the forum, and the court (see Foucault, 1988, especially pp. 63–67). The open institutions do not develop the notion of the private individual, but only the public agent, the citizen, or party to a contract. It is closed institutions that foster the individualizing tactic whose original source Foucault finds in the individualizing drive of the Shepherd.

Foucault thus finds in the metaphor of Christopher the fundamental seed of modernity, just as Tournier finds in Christopher
the seed of the Hitlerian idea of community and ultimately all
metaphoricity. Freud also used the figure of Christopher to make a
point. On two occasions, over the space of thirty years, he made
the same criticism of Bernheim's theory of suggestibility as the
foundation of the practice of hypnotism and thus of all human
collectivity. Freud remembered that:

> . . . my resistance [to Bernheim's theory] took the direction of
> protesting against the view that suggestion, which explained
> everything, was itself to be exempt from explanation. Think-
> ing of it, I repeated the old conundrum:
>
> > *Christoph trug Christum*
> > *Christus trug die ganze Welt,*
> > *Sag'wo hat Christoph*
> > *Damals hin den Fuss gestellt?*
>
> > [Christopher bore Christ;
> > Christ bore the whole world;
> > Say, where did Christopher
> > Then put his foot?]

[Freud, 1921, p. 89]

Freud is demanding that psychoanalysis find a more secure foundation than a concept that has itself no firm foundation. Where
does Christopher's power to carry the world come from? Where
does psychoanalysis' power to transform, to carry, to transfer
come from? Freud's answer was: not suggestion, but transference.
Winnicott's answer was: holding. Winnicott's answer, like Freud's,
comes close to saying that there is a fundamental metaphoricity at
the heart of such answers. What else is transference—the German
Übertragung (from *über tragen*, literally "to carry over")—than a
version of the Greek *meta-phorein*, literally "carrying across"? What
else is holding than the original form of carrying across? In all
fairness, Bernheim might well have riposted: but what does "suggestion" mean but to "to carry under"—from the Latin this time,
"carry (*gerere*) under (*sub*)"? Do we here touch on a phobia specific
to Freud, but one worth taking seriously: his distaste for words
that employ the prefix "under"—*Unterbewusste*, suggestion? As if

there were something underhand about these words, when compared with the honest level movement of *Übertragung* or *Unbewusste*.

Maybe that is the reason why Winnicott left as mysterious what actually happened to Patrick in the water as his father sank under the waves, into oblivion. By holding Patrick, by managing Patrick, his mother, his family, his school—even the passage of time as manifested in the crucial anniversary of his father's death ("With my help the mother and Patrick arranged to be alone together on the afternoon of this the first anniversary of the tragedy, which was also, of course, Patrick's birthday. . . . They sat together all the afternoon and heard the clock tick by. Thus the time passed. Then Patrick said: 'Oh thank goodness that's over, it wasn't half as bad as I thought it was going to be'")—Winnicott made possible the re-experiencing of Patrick's loss of his Christopher, the strong man who carries across the water. Yet the metaphor of Christopher, like the metaphor that underlies psychoanalysis—metaphor, transference, holding—can be only a metaphor. The aim of analysis is to restore to metaphors their metaphoricity: their ability to carry. Because, in the end, Winnicott could hold Patrick only symbolically. As he himself put it, the most important thing that Winnicott could do for Patrick was not impersonate St Christopher, the metaphorical living father. If he had done so, he might have led Patrick into feeling that swimming off by himself would mean the death of the analysis. What Winnicott (see 1954, p. 286) most needed to do was to survive.

CHAPTER THREE

"So rare a wonder'd father": Winnicott's negotiation of the paternal

John Fielding

P *atient:* At times I do feel aware of carrying father around with me. When I say I am angry with myself, I mean that this father is angry with me. When I say I am discussing something with myself, it is this father and I who are discussing. Sometimes I feel almost as if I am my father.

Analyst: The difficulty is that in your memories of your father you are not able to think of him as entering into your world and not even sponsoring it either.

Patient: Mine is a valid criticism of my father. He could never enter into anyone else's world at all. People simply had to go into his world. [Winnicott, 1986]

The "analyst"—Winnicott himself—intervenes here to provide both holding and interpretation. He, characteristically, has heard what the patient has said in all its implications, has "taken it on board"—as might be said now—and travelled with it in his own imagination to the point where he can inhabit the desolation without succumbing to it and so provide the insight that enables the patient to take a further step in his own journey to understanding.

It is striking that the guilty introspection of the patient's first com-ment resolves in the second into anger, which clarifies his sense of his father's lack of imaginative identification.

In this chapter, I should like to tease out the intriguing impli-cations of this fragment of an analysis and to suggest that the often-observed absence of the paternal in Winnicott's theoriza-tion might be illuminated by a consideration of the figure of Prospero in Shakespeare's *Tempest*. The final two sentences quoted above from Winnicott's patient described what happens literally in Shakespeare's play. In order to effect any sort of resolution/ closure/termination, Prospero has to assemble on his island all the people who have impinged on him in the past and subject them to processes that have the foregone conclusion of their greater self-knowledge; they are forced to enter his world. Prospero, through his magic, is altogether in control of what is done to them, and yet it is remarkable that there is no sympathetic identification from him with what they might themselves feel; his concern is that they conform to what he has mapped out for them. Miranda, his daughter, from the first identifies with those in the shipwreck her father has caused: "O I have suffered with those that suffer." To which Prospero's response is the Olympian, "Be collected. No more amazement", and an insistence on his own paternal role, "I have done nothing but in care of thee". We have therefore, at the beginning of the play, an intense focus on a particular father—daughter relationship where the father, in the self-reassurance of an over-arching total—and totally controlled—concern for her, nevertheless has to negotiate a number of very different roles, including the maternal, both towards her and towards his other (substitute) children and "patients"—that is, those he makes suf-fer, who embody, of course, at various times, split-off parts of himself. And, in discussing these questions with himself (even when he is ostensibly talking to other characters, he is actually talking to himself), he evinces a notable inability to enter into their worlds, especially that of his daughter. In this he is just like Winni-cott's patient's father. And, unlike Winnicott's, Prospero's journey (literal, in his case) has been towards a cerebral understanding—an interpretation that precludes holding.

A study of the Prospero–Miranda relationship will lead to an examination of the father's function with regard to the mother/

baby and this will involve an exploration of Winnicott's conceptualization of male/female elements in relation to the father's
function, with special attention to what I take to be Prospero's
hijacking of the maternal, shorn of its nurturing or providing. This
I relate to the split-off function of Caliban as the repository of
linguistic properties significantly absent in Winnicott's conceptualization, and as an embodiment for Prospero of the hateful
aspects of the mother. It is to Caliban's own mother, an absence in
the play, that Prospero attributes a hate that is altogether con-
sonant with the hate for their babies that Winnicott ascribes to
mothers in "Hate in the Countertransference" (1947).

I came first to think about these issues some years ago when
I played Prospero in a school production at the Lycée Français
Charles de Gaulle in London. In the well-established English
tradition of school plays, it was cast according to exigency, cross-
generationally, cross-gender, and, given the nature of the school,
cross-culturally. In rehearsals and in performance, therefore, a
transgressive space was opened up for inhabitation by the play
of difference. That released within the text what felt like an
infinite series of mirror images of parent and child and of the
other relationships that can be mapped onto that—teacher/pupil,
director/actor, analyst/patient, performer/spectator. Indeed, in
rehearsing the scene in which Prospero encourages his daughter to
remember, I wanted Miranda lying on the ground with Prospero
at her shoulder, out of sight, in the classic psychoanalytic configuration. Perhaps fortunately, the girl playing Miranda was having
none of that, and her inability to remember became a refusal to
allow her father into her unconscious—and that turned out to be a
powerful reading in itself.

My own roles felt at times heady in their variety: preparing to
perform the controlling father; while in the classroom teaching the
play academically for A-level to some of the pupil-actors; while
enjoying improvisation with the whole cast, some of them very
young; while taking direction but also intervening to move the
production into areas that I personally wanted it to explore. There
are a number of overlapping transitional spaces here, and, as I
come to articulate these ideas, there is, of course, yet another, a
further mirror image—that of writer/reader. In all of these images
there is the possibility of reading the first term as male and the

second as female, though the text of the play has some difficulty in imposing that on the disruptive imaginings of the "female" that insist on breaking through. The focus of my thinking was then in the connections between mothering and fathering and the combining of these within one person, and that led me to look again at what Winnicott has to say about the paternal function.

It has often been noted that Winnicott assigns a minor role to the father. Adam Phillips, for example, refers to the father as "a relatively bland figure in Winnicott's developmental theory" and observes that Winnicott replaced him with a fascination with the child and its mother. "It is not the father that interests Winnicott as coming between the mother and child to separate them, but a transitional space from which the father is virtually absent" (Phillips, 1988, p. 28). Phillips also points out that Winnicott makes nothing of the connection between the child's acquisition of language and its shift from a two-person to a three-person relationship—a connection that is so crucial to Lacanian theory and so relevant to Caliban's

> You taught me language and my profit on't
> I know how to curse

—where the function of language is seen as an attack on and an enabling of differentiation from the controlling father.

Winnicott's own view of the father's role can be seen as a reduplication of the mother's: as she holds the baby, so he holds her. And it is certainly difficult to find any extended consideration of the way that the father functions in the dynamics of separation. Though Winnicott had read Lacan and used the notion of the "mirror stage" for his own purposes, he refers only fleetingly to the idea that the father's function is a stern and forbidding one and not at all to the association of that with submission to a pre-existing language. Even the title of the chapter in *The Child, the Family and the Outside World*—"What about Father?"—suggests an awareness that the question could be felt to have been marginalized. And that feels a little like Prospero, in the second scene of the play, forestalling Miranda's questions as if he knew they were coming and was prepared for them. Winnicott's formulations in "What about Father?" are in terms of backing up what the mother initiates. If the first function is "protective cover", "the second thing

. . . is that father is needed to give mother moral support, to be the backing for her authority, to be the human being who stands for the law and order which mother implants in the life of the child". The Lacanian perspective is here approached but sidestepped.

> Besides it is much easier for the children to be able to have two parents; one parent can be felt to remain loving while the other is being hated, and this in itself has a stabilizing influence. . . . Every now and again the child is going to hate someone, and if father is not there to tell him where to get off, he will hate his mother, and this will make him confused. [Winnicott, 1964, p. 115]

Miranda, in the play, has only her father, and I think, in this context, of the extraordinary conflict in her, in that second scene, between her desire to attack her father for what he has done to the ship (and for his obliquity in recounting their history) and her utter submission to him, her over-identification with his mood and purpose.

Winnicott continues:

> The third thing to say is that father is needed by the child because of his positive qualities and the things that distinguish him from other men, and the liveliness of his personality. . . . It is hardly possible to begin to describe the ways in which a father enriches the life of his children, so wide are the possibilities. [pp. 115–116]

What strikes one about these passages is how difficult Winnicott finds it to imagine a distinctively masculine role for the father. His imagination is richly focused on what mothers are and do. And, of course, his thesis about psychotherapy is grounded in the analogy between the potential space between mother and child and the playing that is necessary to a fruitful analytic relationship. "Psychotherapy takes place in the overlap of two areas of playing, that of the patient and that of the therapist. Psychotherapy has to do with two people playing together" (Winnicott, 1971a, p. 38). Prospero, on the contrary, has great difficulty with play, both in himself and in others; and, in his imagination, rather than fathering being subsumed in mothering, the reverse has happened. Prospero has been entirely responsible for the nurture and education of Miranda, his only child. Her mother is alluded to only once, glancingly, and then in the context of a characteristically early-modern anxiety about paternity:

> Thy mother was a piece of virtue, and
> She said thou wast my daughter.

Miranda herself shows no curiosity about her and has no memory of her, only of the oddly numerous mother-substitutes who tended her, as if that splitting of the mother disperses the potential for attachment and thereby attenuates its power.

At the beginning of the long, expository second scene of the play, Prospero embarks on an account, to his daughter, of the events that brought him to the island where they have been marooned for twelve years. He needs to explain what it is in his and her history that is to be resolved in the next two hours or so—the play is unusual in the canon in that it faithfully observes the unity of time and constantly reminds us of the passage of those hours. But, before he tells her what he wants her to know, he asks what she remembers of the time before they came to the island—she was not 3 years old when they arrived. Or, rather, he wants to hear that she remembers nothing before the time when he had complete charge of her, for he anticipates her answer:

> Canst thou remember
> A time before we came unto this cell?
> I do not think thou canst, for then thou wast not
> Out three years old.

He is surprised that she does claim a memory.

> *Mir.* Certainly sir I can.
>
> *Pros.* By what? By any other house or person?
> Of anything the image tell me that
> Hath kept with thy remembrance.
>
> *Mir.*   'Tis far off,
> And rather like a dream than an assurance
> That my remembrance warrants. Had I not
> Four or five women once that tended me?
>
> *Pros .* Thou hadst, and more, Miranda. But how is it
> That this lives in thy mind? What seest thou else
> In the dark backward and abysm of time?

There are two sets of phrasing that are interesting here. There is, of course, the idea that it is perhaps a dream rather than a memory which needs to be interpreted; there is free association—"of *anything* the image tell me". And there is some notion, too, of a talking cure, images put into words and spoken to a holding presence in whom is invested complete trust. Prospero at this moment is attempting to calm and contain Miranda's extreme distress at the sight of the shipwreck in which she has felt psychically involved. And Prospero is releasing her from the pain of that by taking her back, intrigued perhaps by an original abandonment or loss.

But there is also some notion of the unconscious. Miranda's images have, as it were, a life of their own. They have "kept with thy remembrance". Not "you have kept them", which is the more standard idea of memory, as a kind of inert filing system, but "they have kept with thy remembrance". They are not identical with your remembrance; only now can they emerge into consciousness. And look for a moment at Prospero's immediate fascination with the process of evoking those memories. "How is it that this *lives* in thy mind?" (though the emphasis is mine, the movement of the verse does enforce a pause over "lives"). These memories have an independent existence within Miranda's mind. "What seest thou else in the dark backward and abysm of time?" The powerful phrasing there evokes the forbidden repressed energies of the id—Prospero is later to call Caliban, his own unacknowledged dark side, "this thing of darkness"—but also the hidden, recessive, infinitely fissured texture of the unconscious. "Backward" implies reversed, inverted, a topsy-turvy opposition to all that is settled, rational, controlled. And "abysm" represents the fantasy of the endless fall into it, the fear of all that may be re-experienced there. For a moment Prospero confronts that, reflected in his daughter's face. But frustratingly, for us, and perhaps for a part of Prospero, the rest is blocked off. Miranda remembers no more, and her father can impose his version of the past and elaborate his own self-analysis.

He does this in a peculiarly convoluted way, not at all adapted to what Miranda might be able to understand, and focused, almost to her exclusion, in his knotted resentments. He entirely occludes his wife and, indeed, in one strong image re-creates himself as Miranda's mother, as having in a psychic sense given birth to her.

He recounts their exile from Milan, cast out to sea in a rotten boat, and Miranda, in a projective identification highly characteristic of her, apologizes for the distress she must have caused him.

> Alack, what
> Trouble was I then to you.

And he replies:

> O a cherubin
> Thou wast that did preserve me. Thou didst smile,
> Infused with a fortitude from heaven,
> When I have decked the sea with drops full salt,
> Under my burden groaned, which raised in me
> An undergoing stomach to bear up
> Against what should ensue.

There are some very strange displacements here that, oddly, call to mind Lady Macbeth destroying her child in fantasy at the very moment that it is creating itself in the mirror of her face because that creation is felt to be threatening to her inner contents.

> I have given suck, and know
> How tender 'tis to love the babe that milks me;
> I would while it was smiling in my face
> Have plucked my nipple from his boneless gums
> And dashed the brains out. . . .

Prospero first reassures Miranda that *she* was the protecting, holding presence. She, by smiling at him, mothered her own father, enabling him, in fantasy, to give birth to her. Prospero imagines himself in labour —"under my burden groaned"—and, sustained by the presence of the child, giving birth to the child— "an undergoing stomach to bear up against what should ensue". The language, which is ostensibly reporting the courage to endure suffering, insistently evokes birth—perhaps even virgin birth—"a cherubin"—"infused with a fortitude from heaven". The father has given birth to the child without the mother, a fantasy of male self-sufficiency. But I think that the strenuousness of the image, the sense that it contains certain meanings that it cannot easily convey, also gives us the feeling that Prospero cannot with ease inhabit that fantasy. He needs to construct himself as the sole author of his own child but cannot comfortably allow his female element expression.

"Creativity and Its Origins" (1971a), in some ways the most dense, elusive, and controversial of Winnicott's writings, seems to illuminate Prospero's inability to *be* for his daughter rather than to *do* for her, despite his insistence that he is also her mother.

> Either the mother has a breast that *is*, so that the baby can also *be* when the baby and mother are not yet separated out in the infant's rudimentary mind; or else the mother is incapable of making this contribution, in which case the baby has to develop without the capacity to be. . . .
>
> (Clinically one needs to deal with the case of the baby who has to make do with an identity with a breast that is active, which is a male element breast, but which is not satisfactory for the initial identity which needs a breast that *is*, not a breast that *does*. Instead of "being like" this baby has to "do like", or to be done to.) [p. 82]

Prospero's insistent control of the speaking in this scene, his unwarranted anxiety about Miranda's listening to what he says, and his defining for her of the space of her replies—he must have taught language to her too, as well as to Caliban—shows how much the Prospero/Caliban split serves as a metaphor for Winnicott's own non-incorporation of the father's structuring function through language, which has been quite elided in Miranda's case. She, unlike Caliban, seems to have acquired language "naturally": that is to say, she has "done like" and Caliban has been "done to".

Earlier in the second scene, however, there is an even more difficult image, in which Prospero shows that he experiences his own femaleness as threatening. He has tried to tell Miranda of the process whereby his brother, Antonio, had taken over the government of Milan, while Prospero himself had retreated to his study and his beloved books, the mastery of which is the source of his magical powers. What is puzzling in this account—for the audience more than for Miranda herself—is the extent to which Prospero accepts responsibility for what happened. He says that he gave over rule to his brother because he had better, more spiritual matters with which to concern himself, but at the same time insists that Antonio took that rule treacherously.

> My trust
> Like a good parent did beget of him
> A falsehood in its contrary as great
> As my trust was.

That seems to be saying, "I, a good father, did beget of him, my brother, the mother, a bad child", with the implication that it is the mother's fault, her bad blood, if the children were bad. The greater the goodness the father inseminates into the mother, the worse she must be, the worse the child turns out—paternal anxiety, indeed.

But the insistence that Antonio was treacherous also calls up doubts in Prospero that he cannot consciously admit to—but which the imagery gives away—about his failure to forestall or guard against that treachery, about his own impotence in that process. This is clear in a curious gender-switching image.

> That now he was
> The ivy which had hid my princely trunk.
> And sucked my verdure out on't.

"My brother parasitically fed on my maleness and turned me into a mother drained by an insatiable child." To be a mother is dangerous, to be available for your child is constantly to be threatened with being emptied.

In "Hate in the Countertransference" (1947—one of the richest of his papers), Winnicott lists some of the reasons why a mother hates her baby, and, as Adam Phillips (1988) notes, "they are all the consequence of his ruthless use of her in the service of his own development" (p. 90). One of the reasons is that the baby "is not magically produced" (Winnicott, 1947, p. 201). But one of Prospero's "babies", Ariel, *was* magically produced, and it is with Ariel that Prospero has the most tender relationship in the play. Another "baby", however, Caliban, had a mother, the one mother repeatedly referred to in the play, who is, for Prospero, unequivocally demonic. Sycorax is "a foul witch", a "blue-eyed hag", a "damned witch" banished from human society for "mischiefs manifold and sorceries terrible to enter human hearing". Unlike Prospero's, in his view, her commands were "so earthy and abhorred" that the delicate Ariel refused to obey them and was imprisoned by her in a cloven pine for twelve years. The demon mother's rage was "unmitigable"; only a father could end the torture.

> It was a torment
> To lay upon the damned, which Sycorax
> Could not again undo. It was mine art
> When I arrived and heard thee, that made gape
> The pine and let thee out.

The vengeful mother's ultimate punishment is permanent imprisonment in a constricting womb. And Prospero here sees himself as the male midwife whose art enables him to effect Ariel's rebirth and as entitled therefore to infinite gratitude. That Prospero's accusation of Sycorax is a projection is made immediately clear when Prospero threatens Ariel, for a much more trivial offence, with a parallel punishment.

> If thou more murmur'st, I will rend an oak
> And peg thee in his knotty entrails till
> Thou hast howled away twelve winters.

What Prospero cannot acknowledge is that he figures as an equivalently hateful mother.

Like her, he uses his control of food as a means of punishment, dramatized in the humiliation of Alonso and his company at the disappearance of the magic banquet just as they move to eat. Prospero himself was thrust forth from Milan and its nourishments, and he here subjects his enemies to a symbolic version of his own ordeal. In his fantasy of Ferdinand, the suitor to his daughter, of whom he wholly approves, he threatens him with a mouth-puckering diet:

> Sea-water shalt thou drink. Thy food shall be
> The fresh-brook mussels, withered roots and husks
> Wherein the acorn cradled.

Noticeably, Prospero is not a generous feeder or provider. We never hear how he and Miranda have fed themselves since their sea-journey twelve years ago. Even at the end of the play, when he invites Alonso and the rest of the court to his cell for the night, all he offers them is rest and the story of his life—which will eat into their rest. One is tempted to associate him with Coriolanus and

those others for whom virtue is synonymous with the refusal of
food. It is one of Caliban's strongest, most unanswerable—and
unanswered—replies that "I must eat my dinner". And one of
Caliban's most engaging features is the relish with which he prom-
ises food to others:

> I prithee, let me bring thee where crabs grow,
> And I with my long nails will dig thee pignuts,
> Show thee a jay's nest and instruct thee how
> To snare the nimble marmoset. I'll bring thee
> To clustering filberts, and sometimes I'll get thee
> Young scamels from the rocks.

Prospero, by contrast, does not have the mother's capacity to provide or the ability to nourish or the impulse to play.

What Prospero identifies with is the power of the father—the
father's almost unfettered power to do and to forbid. So it is not
surprising that he has such pre-eminence in the play. From the
beginning he is in control, in possession of all the relevant knowledge and the ability to turn events according to his plan. In his
conscious total identification with the paternal, there is no room
for need or vulnerability. And yet it is clear that Prospero needs
admiration, even reverence. Though he loves his daughter, her
filial affection and dutifulness are insisted upon. Miranda's collusion in that makes a major contribution to what we might call
Prospero's paternal narcissism, the prevailing sense in him that
there is no worthiness like a father's, no accomplishment or power
like his, and that he, Prospero, is the father *par excellence*. Praise of
Miranda, even from her lover, has a way of redounding to her
father.

> For several virtues
> Have I liked several women, never any
> With me so full soul but some defect she owed
> And put it to the foil. But you, O you
> So perfect and peerless are created
> Of every creature best.

"Created" and "creature" draw attention to Prospero's marvellous
powers, powers of himself to design a peerless woman. Ordinary,
imperfect women are merely born; only his art can produce a
paragon.

That is, of course, Prospero's official version of himself, paternal in its purely positive sense—benign, self-controlled, directing
all the circumstances of life towards harmonious resolution. But
that is achieved—if it is achieved—at some cost. There are psychic
conflicts in Prospero that are by no means as resolved as he would
like them to be or—at the end of the play—pretends to himself that
they are. The limits to his power, which are a constant source of
anxiety and frustration to him, are in the inaccessibility of others'
interior states. He cannot *make* Miranda and Ferdinand fall in
love—though fortunately they do; he cannot *make* Ariel feel the
gratitude and love that Prospero needs; and, most of all, he cannot
make Caliban the submissive, truly civilized subject he feels that he
should be. It is not merely a question of not being omnipotent: he
chafes at his inability to enter into people whom he wants to
change, as he knows, for the better. And even in contemplation of
Ferdinand and Miranda, who have become exactly what he hoped
they would, his understatement makes his inability to share their
happiness poignant.

> So glad of this as they I cannot be,
> Who are surprised with all. But my rejoicing
> At nothing can be more.

There is nothing at which he could rejoice more, but at their merg-
ing he is shut out.

This inability to enter anyone else's world is pervasive. He fails
to understand the process whereby his brother might have found
himself in a position to have to take over the government. He
cannot respond to Miranda's distress at the shipwreck or at his
own, feigned, anger with Ferdinand. He projects onto Ariel the
satisfactions in his work that he ought to have and will not listen
to Ariel's real complaints or recognize how complex Ariel's feelings about him might be. Most crucially, he does not, cannot, hear
Caliban's sensitivity and responsiveness to the realities of the island and to the effects that he himself has wrought:

> Be not afeared. The isle is full of noises,
> Sounds and sweet airs that give delight and hurt not.
> Sometimes a thousand twangling instruments
> Will hum about mine ears, and sometimes voices
> That if I then had waked after long sleep

> Will make me dream again. And then in dreaming
> The clouds methought would open and show riches,
> Ready to drop upon me, that when I waked
> I cried to dream again.

This can certainly be read as an infant perspective, seeing in the clouds a breast symbol and in the riches, the longed-for nurturing milk—in other words, the good breast that Prospero, for all his arrogation to himself of the qualities of the good father, cannot provide.

To be unable to enter anyone else's world must be seriously disabling, even for a father, and it seems to me an extraordinary insight that Shakespeare should know that he could end—not resolve—a play in which these matters have been most intensely explored only by having the central character step outside the play to appeal for the indulgence of the "real" audience to acknowledge both the existence of the play area itself and his own equivocal situation within it.

CHAPTER FOUR

Alone among three: the father and the Oedipus complex

Graham Lee

There is a paradox at the heart of psychoanalysis. It is a field in which we try to use a finite, knowing, public language to fix and make sense of internal experiences that are infinite, private, and perhaps fundamentally unknowable. I am particularly drawn to Winnicott's theories because his model holds this essential paradox at its core. In my view, Winnicott's theory, with its enigmatic focus on the importance of paradox and its sensitive evocation of the mother–infant relationship, is one that approaches, within the confines of descriptive language, the fluid and dynamic experience of human psychological development. Winnicott's model is a psychology of dialectical meanings, a psychology that develops from the infant's experience of merger and oneness in tension with the experience of mother and twoness. In the consulting-room, I readily draw on Winnicott's ideas when I experience myself, in the transference and countertransference, one moment as the patient's symbiotic or narcissistic object and the next as his or her mother (or primary other). Working with such psychological tension or paradox can be a rich and facilitating perspective.

However, what about the experience of the father and of threeness? In spite of the frequent references in his writing to the work of Freud, Winnicott's focus is directed firmly away from the role of the father and an appreciation of the Oedipus complex in psychological development. If, then, I am confronted in the clinical situation with an oedipal transference, must I dispense with Winnicott and look for another theoretical perspective? Or is there a way in which I can link the oedipal to Winnicott's ideas? In view of the important challenge to the apparent absence of the father in much of psychoanalytic theory since Freud (Samuels, 1985, 1989, 1993), I believe that there is a need for an account of the father, the primal scene, and the Oedipus complex in a language that draws upon the subtlety of Winnicott's ideas. In this chapter, I explore ways in which oedipal theory can be used to inform or develop our understanding of Winnicott's model, in particular extending his ideas about the role of paradox.

For Freud, the Oedipus complex is the centrepiece of psychoanalysis, the major principle by which the sexual meanings of human experience are organized. It is in the triangular dynamics of the oedipal situation that the infant experiences sexual desire and sexual difference, and it is the sublimation of incestuous and murderous wishes that forms the basis for the superego and, ultimately, the internalization of morality. As the normal climax of infantile sexual development, the Oedipus complex is an axiomatic step towards psychological health and maturity, and, where neurosis exists, it is the theoretical starting place for understanding and analysis of that neurosis. Following Freud, Klein grappled with the concept of the Oedipus complex and developed her own important and detailed account of oedipal theory. However, Klein's model, with its emphasis on the primitive defence mechanisms and the unconscious phantasies of the infant in relation to its first object (the breast), represents a shift in emphasis from the pivotal concern with the psychological experience of threeness contained in Freud to a greater concern with the psychological experience of twoness. This shift in emphasis within Klein paved the way for Winnicott's theoretical contributions.

Although Winnicott viewed his contribution to psychoanalytic theory as building upon the work of Freud and Klein and he does make reference to the Oedipus complex in many of his papers, his theory is primarily concerned with the relationship between mother and baby. For Winnicott, psychological health depends on the experience of a "good-enough mother", of someone who provides a holding and mirroring environment that maintains the baby's illusion of omnipotence. He further emphasizes the role of the mother in providing appropriately phased disillusionments to the baby's omnipotence, which enables the experience of transitional phenomena in a potential space that is, paradoxically, separateness and not-separateness, and this is the basis for the symbol and symbol usage. Furthermore, the mother secures the move from object relating to object usage by survival and non-retaliation to the infant's destructiveness. If the mother's adaptation is good enough and the infant's omnipotence is met, "the True Self has a spontaneity, and this has been joined up with the world's events" (Winnicott, 1960, p. 146). However, if the mother's adaptation is not good enough, then "the process that leads to the capacity for symbol-usage does not get started (or else it becomes broken up, with a corresponding withdrawal on the part of the infant from advantages gained)" (1960, p. 146). In this circumstance, the defences of the false self develop to take over the caretaking functions that the mother has failed to provide.

The father, as distinct from mother, has no specific role in this conception of early development, for when the father, rather than the mother, attends to the infant, he is only an aspect of the infant's maternal care (Winnicott, 1968b, p. 141). The father is rather vaguely characterized as having a more general role at a later stage in opening up a new world to the children (Winnicott, 1964, p. 116) and as being part of the later strengthening of processes that start up in early infancy in relation to the mother (Winnicott, 1963c, p. 74). Psychopathology stems from the earlier mother–infant relationship, and it follows that psychoanalysis for Winnicott is not primarily concerned with the specific impact of the paternal or the oedipal.

So, how might Winnicott's ideas be extended to the oedipal situation? In order to prepare the ground for exploring this question, I should like to make a theoretical leap to the ideas of Bion and other post-Kleinians, since they provide an example of how a psychology of twoness can be evolved and enriched by a consideration of threeness.

The work of Bion (1962, 1970) resembles that of Winnicott to the extent that both writers emphasize the psychological importance of the mother–infant dyad. Bion introduced the concept of the container and the contained to describe the capacity of the mother to contain the infant's projections, which transforms anxiety and enables the infant to introject the breast as a container capable of dealing with anxiety. Through this process, primitive beta elements are transformed into alpha function, a higher level of the mental process. Thus it is that the experience of a good relationship between container and contained is, for Bion, the basis for the later capacity for thinking and for symbolization. The container–contained first appears in a dyadic situation, between the mother (or breast) and the baby. Thus we might draw a parallel with the capacity to sustain paradox and experience transitional phenomena in Winnicott's work, since each derives primarily from the infant's early experience of the mother.

Bion's concepts have now extended to a consideration of the role of the father and the psychological experience of threeness. Based on the concept of the primal scene (as also used by Klein), Britton (1989) introduces the idea of an oedipal triangle as a bounded space in which there is the possibility of being an observer as well as a participant.

> The acknowledgement by the child of the parents' relationship with each other unites his psychic world, limiting it to one world shared with his two parents in which different object relationships can exist. The closure of the oedipal triangle by the recognition of the link joining the parents provides a limiting boundary for the internal world. [p. 86]

The primal scene conceived of in this way can be viewed as an extension of the concept of the container–contained, with the experience of threeness introducing the possible experience of exclusion. As Segal (1989) phrases it,

> . . . the original relation between container and the contained is the basis of a later concept of the relationship between the penis and the vagina. However, there is an important difference. In the original situation the child is a participant and a beneficiary of that relationship. Recognizing the parental

couple confronts him with a good contained–container relationship from which he is excluded. [pp. 7–8]

According to this theory, the status of the Oedipus complex as represented in the specific sexual contents of the primal scene is directly linked to the development of creativity and thinking (Feldman, 1989, pp. 125-126; Meltzer, 1973, p. 85). The capacity to tolerate the parents coming together will be experienced in the same way as thoughts coming together in the mind. If the anxieties associated with the primal scene are too great, then the capacity to make connections between different parts of the mind will be disrupted.

This model of the primal scene as representing a kind of bounded exclusion from the parental couple, and the potential psychological difficulties associated with this experience, prepares the way for my exploration of the possible links between Winnicott's theory and the concept of the Oedipus complex. This link will be developed through a consideration of Winnicott's ideas about the importance of paradox.

The capacity for paradox

The notion of paradox is central to Winnicott's theory of psychological development, and its role has been amplified by Ogden (1984). Potential space—the space for illusion—results from the sustaining of paradox, and the nature of potential space can be elucidated by considering the paradoxes and the defining poles of the paradoxes (Ogden, 1994, pp. 50–60): the paradox of oneness and twoness in primary maternal preoccupation, the infant's experience of I and me in the mirroring relationship, the creating and discovery of the object in transitional object relatedness, the creative destruction of the object in object usage. It is through paradox that the infant experiences the illusion of omnipotence, of having created what is there to be found, and this experience is the basis for play, creativity, and the use of symbols. For Winnicott, psychological health is underpinned by the paradoxes surrounding the

mother–infant dyad. The role of the father and threeness in relation to the experience of paradox is not really explored.

However, Winnicott provides a link between his emphasis
upon paradox and the concept of the Oedipus complex in his paper, "The Capacity to Be Alone" (1958b). He proposes that the
capacity to be alone, which is ultimately an important aspect of
emotional maturity, is based on a paradox: "it is the experience of
being alone while someone else is present" (Winnicott, 1958b, p.
30). A crucial determinant of the capacity for such paradox is,
according to Winnicott, the toleration of the primal scene.

> It could be said that an individual's capacity to be alone de-
> pends on his ability to deal with the feelings aroused by the
> primal scene. In the primal scene an excited relationship be-
> tween the parents is perceived or imagined, and this is
> accepted by the child . . . who is the third person in a three-
> body or triangular relationship. [1958b, p. 31]

Dealing with the experience of the primal scene and the oedipal
situation represents for Winnicott a significant psychological
achievement. It is here that I want to put forward an idea that I
believe constitutes an extension of Winnicott's theory. I wish to
suggest that the psychological achievement in the oedipal situation, with its pivotal impact on the capacity to be alone, corre-
sponds to a distinct capacity for paradox giving rise to a distinct
kind of potential space. The nature of the paradox and the potential space in the three-person situation is different in some way
from the paradox and potential space of the two-person situation.

In what way, then, might the paradoxes of the two-person situation and of the three-person situation be different? For Winnicott,
the paradox of potential space is based in the infant's experience of
being separate and not-separate from mother; it is the paradox of
oneness and twoness. By contrast, I suggest, the paradox in the
oedipal situation is the experience of exclusion and not-exclusion
from the parents' relationship: it is the paradox of twoness and
threeness. Introducing a corresponding distinction into the notion
of potential space, we can think of the "dyadic potential space" as
referring to the two-person relationship and the "oedipal potential
space" as referring to the three-person relationship.

We can elucidate the nature of these potential spaces by considering the paradoxes, and the defining poles of the paradoxes. In

the case of the dyadic potential space, the poles of the paradox can be described as the experience of merger (oneness), on the one hand, and the experience of difference and separateness (twoness), on the other. In "good-enough" circumstances neither pole is experienced in isolation; there is no resolution of the paradox. It is the dialectical tension between the poles of this paradox, the capacity to sustain merged-separateness, that makes dyadic potential space possible.

In the case of the oedipal potential space, one pole of the paradox is described by the oedipal myth in which the father is murdered and there is an incestuous relationship with the mother (twoness). In this sense, the Oedipus complex can be thought of as a fantasy of "not-exclusion" and as a denial of the primal scene. At the other pole of the paradox, there is the experience of the primal scene, of being the excluded observer of the parental intercourse (threeness). It is the dialectical tension between the poles of the paradox, the capacity to sustain the position of incestuous participant in interplay with that of the excluded observer, that makes oedipal potential space possible. From the infant's perspective, the question of whether the experience is of exclusion or not-exclusion must not be broached, just as the question as to whether a transitional object is me or not-me must remain unformulated (Winnicott, 1953, p. 12).

Potential space, resulting from the sustaining of paradox between fantasy and reality, is the space for illusion, the infant's illusion of omnipotence. In dyadic potential space, the illusion is the infant's creation of the mother (or mother's breast), and this is the forerunner to transitional phenomena, play, and the use of symbols. In a similar way, oedipal potential space can be viewed as an area for illusion, but in this case, I would suggest, the illusion is the infant's creation of the two parents together. This illusion is the basis for a more fully developed conception of the symbol than occurs in the dyadic situation. This view draws on Wright's distinctions between precursors of symbol formation, such as the experience of mother's face within the mother–infant dyad, and full symbolic representation, such as language, which arises in the bounded space created by the oedipal situation (Wright, 1991, pp. 105, 121). It also draws on Lacan's theory that the task in resolving the Oedipus complex is to move beyond the imaginary other (mother) by acquiring the "name-of-the-father", thus recognizing the Symbolic Order and the law of language (Lacan, in Benvenuto & Kennedy, 1986, p. 133). The parents' relationship, created by the infant, can be experienced as a fertile linking together, as two separate thoughts coming together in the mind creating a new thought or a symbol, just as the parents coming together can create a baby.

I would suggest that symbol formation can be viewed as a two-way dynamic between the creative illusions of dyadic and oedipal potential space. It is two-way because, I would argue, the psychological experience is not only of the linear, diachronic developmental sequence of oneness to twoness to threeness. There can be a movement in the opposite direction. For example, once there is a fully fledged symbol, the infant can again experience the notion of twoness—that is, the dyad of infant and symbol. Furthermore, the symbol as the infant's own creation can be experienced as merged with the self, as a kind of oneness.

The dynamic relation between dyadic and oedipal potential space can be illustrated by considering the aspects of creativity that we might associate with each space. The creativity of dyadic potential space is perhaps characterized by an absence of a sense of boundaries, a lack of real-world constraints, and a potentially infinite, free flow of images and ideas. The creativity of oedipal potential space is perhaps characterized by a more bounded linking together of ideas, connecting them to a cultural and historical context and generally taking account of how ideas can be applied within the real world. For example, we might think of the images of free association as created within dyadic potential space, in contrast to psychoanalytic insights as occurring within oedipal potential space. The dynamic between these potential spaces is shown in the fact that not only can free associations contribute to psychoanalytic insight, but psychoanalytic insight can itself give rise to free associations. I should emphasize that the paradox of dyadic and oedipal potential space, and the dynamic between them, is not something that disappears in adulthood. The capacity for paradox, conceived by Winnicott as potential space, is retained throughout life "in the intense experiencing that belongs to the arts and to religion and to imaginative living and to creative scientific work" (Winnicott, 1953, p. 14).

The establishment of oedipal potential space

What, then, are the conditions for the establishment and use of oedipal potential space? I would propose that we think of it as based on the experience of parents, or parental figures, as providing a good-enough handling of the incestuous and aggressive impulses that are associated with the oedipal situation. In using the term "good enough", I am applying Winnicott's idea of the importance of gradual disillusionment by the parents of the infant's omnipotence, as well as the idea of the parents enabling object usage through survival of the infant's attacks. I would emphasize that the experience of the parents as good enough is a result of an interaction between the instinctual impulses of the infant and the capacity of the parents to transform those impulses through their adequate handling. There is a dynamic between instinct and environment. For example, Winnicott notes that the mother's lessening adaptation to her baby follows "her perception of the baby's new need, the need for her to be a separate phenomenon" (1971b, p. 107), and Samuels emphasizes that "babies and mothers have an investment in separation" (1993, p. 141). In a similar vein, I would argue that in the oedipal situation the move towards the infant as excluded is not something that is purely imposed by the environment. The infant has an investment in exclusion as well as the parents.

In the context of good-enough parenting, castration is not a fearful threat that destroys the Oedipus complex, as it is for Freud. Castration as a possibility is an aspect of disillusionment, a component of a gradually less adaptive environmental experience in which there is a growing awareness of the firm boundary between infant and parents. In order to experience a robust boundary in a positive way, the castration possibility must occur in a context of trust and reliability. There must be an image of father as encouraging and affirming, as well as father as barrier. The idea of the positive affirming father is an aspect noted by many writers emphasizing the role of the father outside the specific oedipal configuration, suggesting, for example, the importance of the good-enough or loving father (Blos, 1993, p. 59; Layland, 1985, p. 168) or a distinct kind of paternal reverie and holding that enables a son to move between different styles of aggression (Samuels,

1993, pp. 158–162). In my view, the infant's experience of the paternal dyad, as well as that of the maternal dyad, is likely to have an impact on the establishment of dyadic potential space, and these dyadic relationships will also interact with the experience of threeness and therefore the establishment of oedipal potential space. Thus there will be an interplay between the experience of the oedipal and the dyadic mother. If this interplay is experienced as good enough, it will provide a basis for the illusion of twoness in the presence of threeness and so for the establishment of oedipal potential space.

Dangers in the resolution of paradox

If parenting is not good enough, or indeed if the psychotherapist's handling of the patient is not good enough, there is the danger that paradox will not be sustained, with a consequent collapse in potential space and the use of symbolic thought. We can consider the particular impact of a failure to sustain the paradox of twoness and threeness by first considering the situation of oneness and twoness. Referring to what I have termed dyadic potential space and the paradox of separation and no-separation, Winnicott notes that "the resolution of paradox leads to a defence organization which in the adult one can encounter as true and false self organization" (1953, p. 14). I would suggest that different aspects of the false self organization depend on the particular direction of the resolution of the paradox. If the resolution is towards not-separation, then separation is denied through a fantasy of merger with the "other". This fantasy is manifested as a compliance with the needs and expectations of the "other", as if they belonged to the self. If, on the other hand, the resolution is towards separation, then not-separation is denied through a fantasy of emotional independence, manifested as a lack of neediness or even coldness, a dissociation of mind and emotion that can be characterized by the intellect becoming the location of the false self (Winnicott, 1960, p. 144).

Both poles of the paradox can occur in a false self organization, but there is a denial of tension between the poles. There is a split between the experience of separation and the experience of not-separation. The resolution of paradox leads to a dyadic potential space that is limited or in, some circumstances, dangerous. Its limitations are reflected in a lack of spontaneity, play, and imagination. Its dangerousness is reflected in persecutory experiences resulting from what is injected into the potential space from outside (Winnicott, 1967, pp. 102–103).

In the oedipal situation a failure to sustain the paradox of twoness and threeness, due to prematurely frustrated omnipotence, can result from an experience of prohibition and boundary. In this case, I would argue, the resolution of the paradox of exclusion and not-exclusion is encountered as a fixing of the Oedipus complex as a defensive organization. Different aspects of the Oedipus complex relate to the different poles of the resolved paradox.

If the resolution of the paradox is towards the experience of not-exclusion, then exclusion is denied through the classical fantasy of murder and incest, which might be manifested as a splitting of the parents into good and bad and a collusion with the good parent. If, on the other hand, the resolution is towards the experience of exclusion, perhaps as a result of a premature awareness of the primal scene and threeness, then there can be an emotional withdrawal and denial of sexual and aggressive impulses. This can be manifested as an attitude of intellectual and moral superiority, a kind of puritanism. Both poles of the paradox of exclusion and not-exclusion can occur in the defensive organization of the Oedipus complex, but the psychological dialectic between the poles of the paradox cannot be experienced.

Thus the Oedipus complex, as a normal part of human development, can become a pathological defence organization that defends against the paradox of oedipal potential space. Where this occurs, oedipal potential space, like dyadic potential space, becomes limited, and in some circumstances dangerous. Its limitations are reflected in a loss in the capacity for creativity and symbolization. Its danger is reflected in persecutory or sado-masochistic fantasies resulting from primal-scene images being imposed on the oedipal potential space.

Applying the concept of oedipal potential space to the analytic context, I believe that a therapeutic attitude that sustains a patient's oedipal fantasy in the transference (twoness), in tension with the boundaries that exclude the patient from, for example, the therapist's private life (threeness), can provide the basis for the patient's capacity to bring together ideas, to make links, and to gain insights. Looking at it the other way round, a therapeutic attitude that over-emphasizes either the experience of exclusion and boundaries, perhaps through an overly dry psychoanalytic stance of dispassionate observation and reflection, or that of inclusion, through over-involvement and collusion with the patient, may encourage a defensive resolution of oedipal potential space and so become an obstacle to therapeutic work.

Clinical illustration

J came into therapy because she was experiencing uncontrollable rages when she suspected her boyfriend of looking at and being attracted to other women. She could see that her reaction to his glances towards other women was irrational, but in the grip of her jealousy she found herself out of control and violent. She told me that she thought all men lecherous and untrustworthy and all women potential rivals. So, from the outset, I was alert to the oedipal dimension in my work with her, her desperate craving for certainty in a trusting relationship, but her total conviction that such trust would be blindly idiotic, leading invariably to betrayal and rejection.

In therapy, J came across as highly seductive and flirtatious, and I found it particularly difficult to establish with her what I felt to be an appropriate balance between professionalism and empathy. She would joke and tease, often asking direct questions, even though she knew that I would tend to turn them around and explore with her why she was asking such a question. On one occasion she said in her typically challenging way that men often whistle at her in the street and seem to be undressing her with their eyes. "But you wouldn't do that, would you?" she said. Her question made me feel quite uncomfortable, in one respect inviting a lustful gaze and yet in another respect making me feel like the object of a wolf whistle. I felt the need to impose a boundary, to assert my professional role. I said that I wondered about her need to be looked at and to be desired, and I referred to her manner with me, which, I said, at times could seem quite flirtatious. "In your dreams, ducky", she replied dismissively and went on to generalize about all men being pigs, shallow animals driven by their primitive instincts. She became superior and distant, and I felt as though my comment had precipitated a repetition of an aspect of her habitual style of defence, to be crisply cynical and emotionally withdrawn. She would not allow me to try to make sense of what was going on between us—if anything, seeming more threatened by and defended against my efforts to think.

This interaction illustrates graphically what I have described as the dangers of resolving the paradox of oedipal potential space. In her flirtatious manner and comments, J was enacting an oedipal fantasy of twoness with me, defying the possible exclusion that would accompany an acknowledgement of my professional boundaries and my commitment to factors other than my relationship with her. I think I was eager to place some distance between myself and J as a defence against her seductive impact, not able to think myself, at that moment, about why she needed to relate in this way and to consider kinds of communication that she might be able to use. I believe that my comment was experienced by J as rupturing the intimacy of our twoness, as a kind of castration of her seductive potency. Her defensive response, "in your dreams, ducky", turned the tables, making me the lustful animal for whom she felt belittling disgust. Her emotional and sexual withdrawal made her aloof, superior to the primitive drives that resided in men, and presumably in any consort that would indulge me. She had resolved the paradox of oedipal potential space to the pole of threeness, with herself as the excluded, and indeed disgusted, observer. I believe that my comment at this time encouraged a repetition of her habitual Oedipus complex defence, initially manifesting as a resolution to seductive twoness, but then swinging to a resolution to distanced thirdness. The comment had not enabled her to sustain a tension between our apparent intimacy and her bounded exclusion, and so she was not able to use oedipal potential space for thinking and making links.

I learned that, with J, I needed to allow more time and space for the erotic transference and to avoid premature disillusionment of her need for twoness. Through this process she gradually began to explore the boundaries of our work, to venture towards an experience of threeness that could be excluding without being rejecting, because it was held in tension with her sense of specialness and twoness. For example, when, some time later, I reminded her about a forthcoming break, she said, "So you're going off to have fun somewhere" and then, satirically, "How will you cope without me?" I wondered how I might respond to this. I said, "For you, it seems that if I don't see you, then I won't be able to think about you or wonder about how things are going for you . . . as if out of sight means out of mind." She did not give one of the razor-sharp responses that I had come to expect, but was quiet. She was thinking, and then she said quite slowly and sadly, "My father never remembers my birthday, even if he is reminded a few days before." J was making an important link, and in this session we went on to elaborate the parallels between her experience of her father and her expectations of me; how her impulse, before and after a break, to withdraw emotionally was a defence against the experience of an earlier, paternal rejection. On this occasion, I think she was able to utilize oedipal potential space. The experience of twoness ("how would I cope without her?" "how would she cope without me?"), and the idea of "being thought about", was held in dialectical tension with threeness and exclusion ("you're going off to have fun somewhere"). My comment did not refer directly to her dependency—I think that might have emphasized exclusion too much. Instead, the idea of her presence in mind invited a sense of twoness and inclusion that she was able to hold in dynamic with the experience of thirdness evoked by the imminent break. She was able to bring together two ideas, to link the memory of her father's forgetfulness and the concern about the break in therapy, and to create an insight for herself—to see how she wanted to withdraw from me for fear of being rejected and hurt. The sustaining of the paradox of oedipal potential space had enabled her capacity to think.

Concluding comments

The concept of oedipal potential space extends Winnicott's idea of the central importance of paradox beyond the mother–infant dyad, to include the role of the father and the experience of threeness in psychological development. The oedipal situation is, according to this view, not only concerned with sexual difference and the nature of incestuous and rivalrous impulses, but also fundamental in the development of the capacity to think. It is in oedipal potential space, generated by the paradox of twoness and threeness, that the infant creates the illusion of the parents together, and this fertile linking is the forerunner for the linking of ideas and ultimately for full symbolic thought. This extension of Winnicott's theory provides a bridge between his emphasis on the mother–infant relationship and Freud's focus on the oedipal situation.

A consequence of the idea of oedipal potential space is a revisioning of Freud's notion of the resolution of the Oedipus complex. The Oedipus legend is a fantasy of twoness through the removal of the unwanted third, and as such it represents one pole of the oedipal paradox—that of not-exclusion. The establishment and use of oedipal potential space is based on the tension between the classical oedipal fantasy of twoness and the realization of threeness through the experience of exclusion evoked by the primal scene. In this sense, in normal development the Oedipus complex is never resolved. Within Winnicott's theory there is no resolution of the fantasy of merger; the fantasy is retained as one pole of the paradox of what I have called dyadic potential space. In a similar way, there is no resolution of the oedipal fantasy of twoness; it is retained as one pole of the paradox of oedipal potential space.

In the psychotherapeutic situation, I have found Winnicott's notion of paradox to be an important concept for maintaining flexibility, movement, and a spirit of inquiry in my work with patients. The idea of oedipal potential space suggests how we might extend and use Winnicott's ideas about paradox in relation to oedipal material.

CHAPTER FIVE

"If father could be home . . ."

Val Richards

G rieving at the lack of physical warmth with his mother, a patient reflected: "If I were to embrace her, it would be like embracing a ghost. I would go right through her. But my *father*, he was solid, he was there. I remember raging earache one night and him carrying me through the streets on his shoulder in search of a hospital." "So you felt held by him?" suggested the therapist. "No!" he cried urgently: "*I* was holding *him*. I could get hold of him and grasp him tightly and rub my face against his jacket. I could clasp him and hug him and pummel him and there he would still be, solid and strong and warm."

The relationship between father and child evoked here serves to introduce the theme of this chapter: the interplay in Winnicott's thought between varieties of holding, as the child's horizons extend to take in the contribution of the father. Both progression and simultaneity are involved. The regime of the father does not *replace* the tender, attuned mother of infancy. Rather than specifically gendered figures, we are faced with a widening pool of qualities, which come into play as the child develops. More than gender, it is the qualities that count. In the above illustration, the father's

---

The title is taken from Winnicott (1945).

masculine ability, like St Christopher (cf. chapter two), to carry the child aloft through the dark night apparently mattered less than his capacity to accept, respond to, yet withstand his son's rough affection, which this particular "ghost"-like mother failed to arouse.

The incident also suggests that, for the growing child, if holding is to be effective, parent and child need equally both to hold and also to be held. *To be held, you also have to hold.* And in his conceptualization, Winnicott sees the father's task as an extension of the original mother–infant holding.

From the early stage of "double dependence" (Winnicott, 1959, p. 138) and a facilitating environment associated primarily with a single figure—mother—the child soon passes to an environment that is made of sterner stuff, to include a *framework*, a climbing frame, for the exploring child to grip, ascend, and be supported by—above all, to be sufficiently durable to withstand assault. This framework is largely associated with the father, who must first of all serve as a buffer between mother and the disruptive child, as a catalyst for their restoration to one another.

> When a child steals sugar, he is looking for the good mother, his own, from whom he has a right to take what sweetness is there. In fact this sweetness is his, for he invented her and her sweetness out of his own capacity to love, out of his own primary creativity, whatever that is. He is also looking for his father, one might say, who will protect mother when she is found. [Winnicott, 1946, p. 116]

Only when the strict and strong father figure is in evidence can the child regain his primitive love impulses, his sense of guilt, and his wish to mend. This father, then, must be "strict and strong" *before* he can be "loving". He must be content at first to play second fiddle to the mother and child, who, needing to make reparation to his/her mother for the sweet theft of the sugar, is "also looking for his father, one might say, who will protect mother when she is found".

As well as mutual playing in harmony and accord, parental holding therefore involves, maybe, restraining, holding on, *holding back*, struggling against. And, as is central to Winnicott's thought, it also actually issues from the vital capacity of parents and children to hate each other (Winnicott, 1947, p. 201), and it leads to the child's impulse to destroy (Winnicott, 1971c, p. 89). Finally, holding implies the cessation of holding, and letting go. Such variations of holding require both the enfolding of the maternal and the "strict, strong" grip of the paternal.

It is the momentum of this paternal aspect of holding that propels Winnicott beyond the expansive "world enough and time" of a long psychoanalytic treatment, and the magical one-off consultations with disturbed children, far into the outside world of magistrates, judges, schools, hostels for delinquents, and, indeed, prisons. To a wide range of audiences, he stressed how the enfolding arms of the mother extend into the strong arms of father, family, school, and, for many, the law:

> The child provokes total environmental reactions, as if seeking an ever-widening frame, a circle which had as its first example the mother's arms or the mother's body. [Winnicott, 1956, p. 125]

With the advent of the father, family love undergoes not a contraction but an expansion into a space (cf. chapter four) and a framework, for which "home" is both the literal name and also symbolic of the equivalent internal space. From here, the child begins to think and link and to "challenge the parents' language, to be, one might say, a bad enough child" (Wright, 1984, p. 99); for, as Winnicott concurs, "If the home can stand up to all the child can do to disrupt, he settles down to play, but first the test must be made. The child needs to be conscious of a framework if he is to feel free" (Winnicott, 1946, p. 115).

Without both forms of holding—the maternal enfolding and the strong paternal grasp—the inevitable early slings and arrows suffered by any fledgling might lead to later disturbance or delinquency. Indeed, with the perils inherent in early development, as depicted by Winnicott, it is remarkable that anyone makes it to psychological maturity:

> The early stages of emotional progress are full of potential conflict and disruption. The relationship to external reality is not firmly rooted. The personality is not yet well integrated. Primitive love has a destructive aim, and the child has not yet learned to cope with instincts. Hence the vital necessity of

home as a strong containing framework and if the frame
breaks, far from enjoying his so-called freedom, he no longer
feels free. . . . Unless he gets into trouble, the delinquent can
only become more and more inhibited in love, and conse-
quently more and more depressed and depersonalised, and
eventually unable to feel the reality of things at all, except the
reality of violence. [Winnicott, 1946, p. 115]

When the framework is too weak, this evokes the most intense
distress and isolation in the alienated, unheld child. For it is the
timely intervention of the father and his provision of a strong
framework which may prevent or curb such a downhill path.
As portrayed in the following extract from *The Piggle* (Winnicott,
1977), the paternal role appears crucial in reversing the effects
of a crisis following the birth of a sibling. The account involves
the regression of a small girl who has been suffering from night
terrors. The sequence portrays a versatility and flexibility of paternal function, in the collaboration between Winnicott and the
actual father, occasioning the child's opportunity to re-enact her
first parental identifications. By playing their appointed parts in
the Piggle's drama as "baby" (Winnicott) and "mother" (actual
father), Winnicott and the real father are handling, holding, and
containing her disturbance and her own culminating pretend birth
as a new baby.

> *Piggle*: Now the Winnicott baby has all the toys. I'll go to
> Daddy.
> *Me*: You are afraid of the greedy Winnicott baby, the baby
> that was born out of Piggle and that loves the Piggle and
> that wants to eat her.

She went to her father and tried to shut the door as she left. I
heard the father working overtime in the waiting room trying
to entertain her, because (of course) he did not know where he
was in this game.

I told the father to come into the room now, and the Piggle
came in with him. He sat in the blue chair. She knew what
must be done. She got on his lap and said: "I am shy."

After a while she showed her father the Winnicott baby,
this monster she had given birth to, and it was this that she
was shy about. . . . Then she started a new and very deliberate

chapter in the game. "I'm a baby too," she announced, as she came out head first onto the floor between her father's legs.

. . . She went on being born from her father's lap onto the floor, and she was the new baby and I had to be cross, being the Winnicott baby that came out of the inside and was born out of the Piggle—and I had to be very cross wanting to be the only baby.

. . . She was now having a different way of being born out of the top of the father's head.* . . . I felt sorry for father, and I asked him if he could stand it. He replied: "O.K., but I would like to take my coat off." He was so hot. However, we were able to finish at this point because the Piggle had got what she came for.

*Being conceived of, i.e. born as an idea in the mind; wanted. D.W.W.

[1977, pp. 28–31]

While Winnicott's primary task appears to have been that of empathic and imaginative facilitator, it is these very powers that reveal him as masterminding the whole show, with the real father assigned a more passive role (cf. Introduction herein). For the real father's main function was both to *stand* and withstand his daughter's onslaught, which mimicked the infant's graduation from wordless primary unity to the mindfulness of the oedipal stage, as indicated in Winnicott's footnote to the extract: "Being conceived of, i.e. born as an idea in the mind; wanted."

The Piggle was indeed fortunate in her opportunity, by virtue of her father's co-operation, to recover a temporarily lost equilibrium. Indeed, it is conceivable that the mere fact of the father's exclusive attention in bringing the Piggle to the session proved therapeutic, compensating for the cut in her ration since the sister's birth.

This shared intervention by Winnicott and the Piggle's father at the Piggle's stage of "relative dependence" (Winnicott, 1963d, p. 87) relates to Winnicott's theory that disturbance and deprivation occurring in this phase can be the source of subsequent delinquency or at least of "anti-social tendencies". Indicators of these may take the form of regressive behaviour, such as messing and bed-wetting, which are at first accepted by the mother as proper to infancy, but later become reactivated for their maximum nuisance value. As a possible reaction to the loss of an earlier, so far unrecovered, good, such symptoms represent the individual's hope of recovering this good.

In the antisocial trends identified by Winnicott, there are two principal manifestations. Stealing is the first—in the hope of regaining the loved and lost object. The other is destructiveness—in the search for a containing environment. For the child has kicked against the framework and the walls have collapsed. The youngster's delinquency masks a quest for the lost and loved internal home of infancy, for the strong-enough unfound father.

It is the failure of the *framework/father* to hold and contain the child, to keep an internal roof over the child's head, that drives him or her to

> . . . become anxious and start to seek for a framework elsewhere than at home . . . for the four walls; he still has hope, and he looks to grandparents, uncles and aunts, friends of the family, school. For he seeks an external stability without which he may go mad. [Winnicott, 1946, p. 117]

Again, it is Winnicott's attunement to the desperation behind such acting out in children that inspires this extension of the paternal function. Failing to hold the child first time around, this father mutates into successively more impregnable, intractable forms for the secure containment of the offender:

> Children deprived of home life must either be provided with something personal and stable when they are yet young enough to make use of it to some extent, or else they must force us later to provide stability in the shape of an approved school or in the last resort four walls in the shape of a prison cell. [p. 119]

This "last resort" of "four walls in the shape of a prison cell" is invoked for offenders who fall into the category of showing a tendency towards depersonalization and dissociation, towards feeling real only in some violent act. Although so compressed, the statement captures the subjectivity of those who expect to be seen only as objects or who perceive others only as objects, as functions of their own fantasy. It charts the progression from self-protection

by means of splitting—"depersonalization and dissociation"—
towards a "violent act", to alleviate feelings of alienation and
unrealness. The offenders attack inanimate targets, they injure
themselves or other people. And, having expelled their own
capacities for feeling into these targets outside themselves, they are
enabled to feel a vicarious "realness" by means of their victims'
pain or killing.

The treatment for delinquents, who may have destroyed their
too–fragile father/framework, who may have harmed themselves,
and others, but have not yet killed, is not the "welcome" four walls
of a prison cell, but the residential home, with carefully selected
staff. In his portrayal of "Residential Care as Therapy" (1970b),
Winnicott emphasizes the therapeutic part played, not only by
these suitably skilled and empathic care workers, but also by the
actual details and reliable structuring of the setting.

> Rather quickly I learnt that the therapy was being done by the
> institution, by the walls and the roof; by the glass conserva-
> tory which provided a target for bricks, by the absurdly large
> baths for which an enormous amount of precious wartime
> coal had to be used up if the water was to reach up to the
> navel of the swimmers. [p. 221]

Here the not irrecoverably damaged child, through this extension
of parental holding, "rediscovers in the institutional environment
a good enough holding situation which got lost or broken up at a
certain stage" (1970b, p. 225).

This combination of human and environmental factors, making up a strong-enough substitute parental setting, is reflected in
the clinical material below, which illustrates also how there can be
an illusion that the enfolding, *holding arms* of one-to-one therapy
may stretch to encompass places beyond the consulting-room, as
the ever-widening circles of holding seemed, quite unwilled, to be
exemplified in the analytic work.

> Max, the child borne on his father's shoulders, as quoted at the
> beginning of this chapter, was director of a new inner-city cen-
> tre for disturbed children. For a whole year before the actual
> arrival of the flesh-and-blood children, he had shared with
> the therapist his "pregnancy"—all the meticulous and detailed

planning, with colleagues, involving the construction of a framework that was intended to hold the pupils, to contain them, in what Max saw as an almost foolproof way. At any sign of trouble, the "system" would be activated, the stages of the procedures set in motion. Of special interest in relation to parental holding was the fact that, while the ultimate deterrent in the sanctions process would be temporary exclusion of the offender, it was only in the most exceptional of circumstances that any strong physical restraint would be used. The main reason for this was that some children are so "touch hungry", so craving to hold and be held, that they become adept at bringing about violent situations in order to get this measure invoked.

Sometimes it sounded to the therapist almost as though these plans were invested with magical powers and might even work without the presence and intervention of human beings/ staff. It felt as though Max were preparing a holding environment in which the alive adults could, somehow, shelter behind the strong bars of the cot that they had built for the expected baby, without the need for the central decisive factor: full, direct contact between the alive adults and the children.

As the first batch of children arrived, it was as if Max were in a state of maternal omnipotence—Winnicott's "primary maternal preoccupation". Because the "labour" had been so thorough, nothing could go wrong after the birth of the actual "baby". At the end of his first week, Max arrived at his session exhausted but euphoric. The week really had gone well, despite a few blips. Even though staff members had seemed over-concerned about children's unruly behaviour, Max had reassured them—the staff had only to be "good enough". They should be more relaxed. Indeed, Max himself—unready, as it were, for the intervention of a "father" figure—had been extremely annoyed by a nosy parent who reported to him that he had seen a boy attempting to climb out of a second-floor window. And it was far more the man's *interference* with Max's holding of this baby than the child's grave danger that had affected Max, in his initial euphoria and total absorption in his task.

As the weeks passed, so did Max's euphoria. He was bringing the whole burden of his anxieties to sessions. Sometimes the weight of this baby, which, he felt, he was holding single-handed, proved unbearable. Then, as the father/framework of the centre became strong enough, it was that very direct, dangerous involvement with individual youngsters and staff that proved transforming. In experiencing a whole range of emotions towards his charges and colleagues, and in closely monitoring these, Max found new pathways opening up in his relationships. Gradually, he felt he could begin to lean back on the reliability of the total organization and allow what he felt to be his "self" to come back into his therapy sessions, and to speak of that now dead, once good-enough father, whom Max could hold as he was held.

REFERENCES

Benvenuto, B., & Kennedy, R. (1986). *The Works of Jacques Lacan*. London: Free Association Books.

Bion, W. R. (1962). *Learning from Experience*. London: Karnac Books, 1984.

Bion, W. R. (1970). *Attention and Interpretation*. London: Karnac Books, 1984.

Blos, P. (1993). "Son and Father." In: *The Gender Conundrum* (ed. D. Breen). London: Routledge.

Britton, R. (1989). "The Missing Link: Parental Sexuality in the Oedipus Complex." In: J. Steiner (Ed.), *The Oedipus Complex Today*. London: Karnac Books.

Casement, P. (1982). "Some Pressures on the Analyst for Physical Contact during the Reliving of an Early Trauma." *International Review of Psycho-Analysis, 9*. Also in: *On Learning from the Patient*. London: Tavistock, 1985.

Eagleton, T. (1985). *Literary Theory: An Introduction*. Oxford: Blackwell.

Feldman, M. (1989). "The Oedipus Complex: Manifestations in the Inner World and the Therapeutic Situation." In: J. Steiner (Ed.), *The Oedipus Complex Today*. London: Karnac Books.

Foucault, M. (1988). "Politics and Reason." In: L. D. Kritzman (Ed.),

Michel Foucault: Politics, Philosophy, Culture: Interviews and Other Writings 1977-1984 (pp. 57–85). New York/London: Routledge.

Freud, S. (1895). *Project for a Scientific Psychology. S.E. 1.*

Freud, S. (1910). *Leonard da Vinci and a Memory of his Childhood. S.E. 11.*

Freud, S. (1920). *Beyond the Pleasure Principle. S.E. 18.*

Freud, S. (1921). *Group Psychology and the Analysis of the Ego. S.E. 18.*

Layland, W. R. (1985). "In Search of a Loving Father." In: A. Samuels (Ed.), *The Father: Contemporary Jungian Perspectives.* London: Free Association Books.

Mannoni, M. (1967). *The Child, His "Illness", and the Others.* London: Tavistock, 1970. [Reprinted London: Karnac Books, 1987.]

Meltzer, D. (1973). *Sexual States of Mind.* Strath Tay, Perthshire: Clunie Press.

Ogden, T. H. (1994). *Subjects of Analysis.* London: Karnac Books.

Phillips, A. (1988). *Winnicott.* London: Fontana.

Phillips, A. (1995). *Terrors and Experts.* London: Faber.

Samuels, A. (Ed.) (1985). *The Father: Contemporary Jungian Perspectives.* London: Free Assocation Books.

Samuels, A. (1989). *The Plural Psyche.* London: Routledge.

Samuels, A. (1993). *The Political Psyche.* London: Routledge.

Segal, H. (1989). "Introduction." In: J. Steiner (Ed.), *The Oedipus Complex Today.* London: Karnac Books.

Tournier, M. (1970). *Le Roi des Aulnes.* Paris: Gallimard.

Winnicott, D. W. (1945). "Home Again." In: *Deprivation and Delinquency.* London: Tavistock, 1984. [Reprinted London: Routledge, 1992.]

Winnicott, D. W. (1946). "Some Psychological Aspects of Juvenile Delinquency." In: *Deprivation and Delinquency.* London: Tavistock, 1984 [Reprinted London: Routledge, 1992.]

Winnicott, D. W. (1947). "Hate in the Countertransference." In: *Through Paediatrics to Psychoanalysis.* London: Hogarth Press, 1975. [Reprinted London: Karnac Books, 1992.]

Winnicott, D. W. (1953). "Transitional Objects and Transitional Phenomena." In: *Playing and Reality.* London: Tavistock, 1971.

Winnicott, D. W. (1954). "Metapsychological and Clinical Aspects of Regression within the Psycho-Analytical Set-Up." In: *Through Paediatrics to Psycho-Analysis.* London: Hogarth Press, 1975. [Reprinted London: Karnac Books, 1992.]

Winnicott, D. W. (1956). "The Antisocial Tendency." In: *Deprivation and Delinquency*. London: Tavistock, 1984. [Reprinted London: Routledge, 1992.]

Winnicott, D. W. (1958a). "Child Analysis in the Latency Period." In: *The Maturational Processes and the Facilitating Environment*. London: Hogarth Press, 1965. [Reprinted London: Karnac Books, 1990.]

Winnicott, D. W. (1958b). "The Capacity to Be Alone." In: *The Maturational Processes and the Facilitating Environment*. London: Hogarth Press, 1965. [Reprinted London: Karnac Books, 1990.]

Winnicott, D. W. (1959). "Classification: Is There a Psycho-Analytic Contribution to Psychiatric Classification?" In: *The Maturational Processes and the Facilitating Environment*. London: Hogarth Press, 1965. [Reprinted London: Karnac Books, 1990.]

Winnicott, D. W. (1960). "Ego Distortion in Terms of True and False Self." In: *The Maturational Processes and the Facilitating Environment*. London: Hogarth Press, 1965. [Reprinted London: Karnac Books, 1990.]

Winnicott, D. W. (1961). "Varieties of Psychotherapy." In: *Home Is Where We Start From*. Harmondsworth: Penguin, 1986.

Winnicott, D. W. (1963a). "Communicating and Not Communicating Leading to a Study of Certain Opposites." In: *The Maturational Processes and the Facilitating Environment*. London: Hogarth Press, 1965. [Reprinted London: Karnac Books, 1990.]

Winnicott, D. W. (1963b). "Dependence in Infant-Care, in Child-Care, and in the Psycho-Analytic Setting." In: *The Maturational Processes and the Facilitating Environment*. London: Hogarth Press, 1965. [Reprinted London: Karnac Books, 1990].

Winnicott, D. W. (1963c). "The Development of the Capacity for Concern." In: *The Maturational Processes and the Facilitating Environment*. London: Hogarth Press, 1965. [Reprinted London: Karnac Books, 1990.]

Winnicott, D. W. (1963d). "From Dependence Towards Independence in the Development of an Individual." In: *The Maturational Processes and the Facilitating Environment*. London: Hogarth Press, 1965. [Reprinted London: Karnac Books, 1990.)

Winnicott, D. W. (1964). *The Child, the Family and the Outside World*. London: Penguin.

Winnicott, D. W. (1965). "A Child Psychiatry Case Illustrating Delayed Reaction to Loss." In: *Psycho-Analytic Explorations*. London: Karnac Books, 1989.

Winnicott, D. W. (1967). "The Location of Cultural Experience." In: *Playing and Reality*. London: Tavistock, 1971.

Winnicott, D. W. (1968a). "Physical and Emotional Disturbances in an Adolescent Girl." In: *Psycho-Analytic Explorations*. London: Karnac Books, 1989.

Winnicott, D. W. (1968b). "Contemporary Concepts of Adolescent Development and Their Implications for Higher Education." In: *Playing and Reality*. London: Tavistock, 1971.

Winnicott, D. W. (1970a). "Cure." In: *Home Is Where We Start From*. Harmondsworth: Penguin, 1986.

Winnicott, D. W. (1970b). "Residential Care as Therapy." In: *Deprivation and Delinquency*. London: Tavistock, 1984. [Reprinted London: Routledge, 1992.]

Winnicott, D. W. (1971a). *Playing and Reality*. London: Tavistock.

Winnicott, D. W. (1971b). "The Place Where We Live." In: *Playing and Reality*. London: Tavistock.

Winnicott, D. W. (1971c). "The Use of an Object and Relating through Identifications." In: *Playing and Reality*. London: Tavistock.

Winnicott, D. W. (1977). *The Piggle*. London: Hogarth Press. [Reprinted Harmondsworth: Penguin, 1980.]

Winnicott, D. W. (1986). *Holding and Interpretation: Fragment of an Analysis*. London: Hogarth Press and the Institute of Psycho-Analysis. [Reprinted London: Karnac Books, 1989.]

Wright, E. (1984). *Psychoanalytic Criticism*. London/New York: Methuen.

Wright, K. (1991). *Vision and Separation: Between Mother and Baby*. London: Free Association Books.

INDEX

Layland, W. R., 81
Lee, G., ix, 8, 73–87
loss:
    object-, theory of, 50
    traumatic, 9, 50
love impulses, primitive, and role of
        strict and strong father, 1, 90,
        91

manic defence, and separation
        anxiety, 27
Mannoni, M., 4, 5, 6
maternal holding, primary, 1
maturational process, family
        function in, 55
Max [case study: strong, holding
        environment], 95–97
Meltzer, D., 77
Melville, H., 51
metaphor:
    meaning of, 53
    and perversion, 54
Miranda [*The Tempest*], 7, 60–71
mirror:
    maternal, 5, 66, 75, 77
    /milk experience, primal, 2, 4
    stage [Lacan], 62
Moby Dick [Melville], 51
Moore, H., 12
mother:
    adaptation of, 75
    containing function of, 76
    disillusioning role of, 75
    dyadic, 82
    good-enough, 75
    hate for baby of, 61, 68
    hateful aspects of, 61, 69
    –infant dyad, 73, 78, 79, 87
        importance of, 76
    internalization of, and symbol
        formation, 2
    oedipal, 82
    separation from, as threat to
        continuity, 55

symbolic, 4
    wood as symbol for, 55
murder, classical fantasy of, 83

narcissism, paternal, 70–71
National Health Service, 47
necrophilia, 54
neurosis, 74

object usage:
    creative destruction of object in, 77
    parents' enabling of, 81
oedipal myth, 79
oedipal situation:
    paradox of, 78
    triangular dynamics of, 74
Oedipus complex, 73–87
    and language, 3
    resolution of, 87
Ogden, T. H., 77
omnipotence:
    abrogation of, 56
    baby's illusion of, 75, 77, 81
        as space for illusion, 79
    maternal, state of, 96
    prematurely frustrated, 83

paedophilia, 51, 54
paradox:
    capacity for, 77–80
        and potential space, 78
    importance of, 73
    resolution of, dangers in, 82–84
    role of, 73–87
pathological defence organization,
        Oedipus complex as, 83
Patrick [case study: delayed reaction
        to loss], 6, 7, 9–40
    Winnicott's management of, 41–
        58
perversion:
    and metaphor, 54
    sexual, 54
Phillips, A., 3, 54, 62, 68